# CRETE

NICK HANNA

NEW HOLLAND

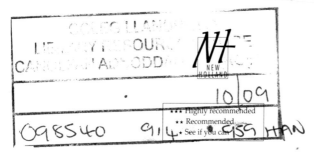

This edition first published in 2000
by New Holland Publishers (UK) Ltd
London • Cape Town • Sydney • Auckland
First published in 1996
10 9 8 7 6 5 4 3 2 1

24 Nutford Place
London W1H 6DQ
United Kingdom

80 McKenzie Street
Cape Town 8001
South Africa

14 Aquatic Drive
Frenchs Forest, NSW 2086
Australia

218 Lake Road
Northcote, Auckland
New Zealand

ISBN 1 85974 475 3

**Commissioning editor**: Tim Jollands
**Manager Globetrotter Maps**: John Loubser
**Editors**: Mary Duncan, Beverley Jollands
**Cover Design**: Éloïse Moss
**Design**: Philip Mann
**Cartographer**: Carl Germishuys

Typeset by Philip Mann, ACE Ltd
Reproduction by Hirt & Carter (Cape) Cape Town
Printed and bound in Hong Kong by Sing Cheong
Printing Co. Ltd.

**Photographic credits:**
**Shirley Arnold**: pages 22, 25, 26, 90, 92, 106; **Jill Birch**: pages 28, 103, 114; **Michael R. Chandler**: pages 12, 54, 94; **Paul Harcourt Davies**: pages 8, 9, 11, 115, 117; **Footprints**: pages 1, 15, 18, 19, 29, 30, 31, 35, 36, 37, 40, 47, 48, 55, 57, 62, 67, 69, 70, 72, 74, 75, 78, 79, 81, 86, 89, 107, 109, 110, 111, 113, 116; **Jeff Goodman**: page 23; **George Grigoriou/Gallo Images**: cover; **Museum of Iráklion**: pages 14, 16, 17, 38, 39, 46, 58; **Andrew Linscott**: page 68; **I. Meredith**: pages 96, 97, 118; **Stuart Morris**: pages 7, 32, 44; **Andreas Nicola**: pages 24, 50, 104, 108; **PictureBank Photo Library**: pages 4, 6, 20, 27, 53, 84, 100; **Valerie M. Whitchelo**: pages 10, 65, 73, 76.

Although every effort has been made to ensure
accuracy of facts, and telephone and fax numbers
in this book, the publishers will not be
held responsible for changes that occur at the time of
going to press.

**Front cover**: *Réthimnon harbour.*
**Title page**: *A village* kafeníon.

# CONTENTS

**1. Introducing Crete 5**
The Land **6**
History in Brief **12**
Government and Economy **22**
The People **24**
Food and Drink **28**

**2. Iráklion 33**
Exploring the City **34**
The Archaeological Museum **38**

**3. Central Crete 45**
Knossós **46**
West of Iráklion **50**
East of Iráklion **52**
Phaistós, Górtyn and the
South Coast **55**

**4. Eastern Crete 63**
Áyios Nikólaos **64**
The Lasíthi Plateau **69**
Sitía and the Far East **74**
Ierápetra **80**

**5. Réthimnon Province 85**
Réthimnon **86**
East of Réthimnon **89**
Mount Psilorítis and
the Amári Valley **92**
The South Coast **95**

**6. Western Crete 101**
Haniá **102**
Akrotíri **106**
Rodhópou **108**
The West Coast **110**
The Samariá Gorge **113**
The South **117**

**Travel Tips 122**

**Index 127**

# 1
# Introducing Crete

Greeks habitually refer to Crete as *megáli nisí*, 'the big island', and indeed it is in many ways a country within a country, with its own character and traditions.

Crete offers all the essentials for the perfect holiday destination: it has resorts as sophisticated as you could wish, miles of beaches (especially on the north coast), a summer which lasts longer than anywhere else in Europe and friendly tavernas where you can laze away the day gazing out across the sparkling Aegean Sea.

But it is the 'added ingredients' which make Crete special, a place apart from any other Greek island. Its highly varied landscapes encompass mighty mountain ranges, fertile plateaux, secluded villages and hidden coves and beaches. In spring, the meadows display a glorious profusion of wild flowers while snow still lies on the rugged peaks above. Best of all, it has a unique island culture, shaped by centuries of civilization.

Crete was the birthplace of European civilization, the home of the Minoans who prospered centuries before classical Greece. They existed only in myth until excavations unveiled the reality of this advanced and cultured society. The remains of their splendid palaces and the displays of their numerous, refined artworks are a major drawcard for visitors to the island.

At the crossroads of the eastern Mediterranean, Crete came under the successive rules of the Greeks, the Romans, the Byzantine Empire, the Venetians and the Turks. Each era has left its mark, creating a colourful, multilayered tapestry of history waiting to be explored.

**TOP ATTRACTIONS**

**\*\*\* Knossós**: The greatest Minoan palace of all.
**\*\*\* Phaistós**: The second most important Minoan palace, in a spectacular setting.
**\*\*\* Iráklion Archaeological Museum**: The legacy of the Minoans in art and artefacts from centuries past.
**\*\*\* Haniá**: Venetian and Turkish influences abound in the old town and harbour of this delightful city.
**\*\* Réthimnon**: Characterful old port with a rich past.
**\*\* Samariá Gorge**: Europe's longest gorge, the most popular day trip on the island.

**Opposite**: *Watching the world go by: the Cretan way of life is relaxed and easy-going.*

## LONGEST AND TALLEST

**Highest mountain: Mount Ídha** in the Psilorítis Range, whose peak stands at 2456m (8057ft). Just 3m lower, the top of Páhnes in the Lefká Óri comes second at 2453m (8048ft).

**Longest river**: the **Yeropótamos**, which winds westwards across the broad Messará Plain for around 45km (28 miles) before disgorging into the Libyan Sea.

**Longest gorge**: **Samariá**, which runs for 17km (11 miles) from the heart of the Lefká Óri and descends 1200m (4000ft) to the sea on the south coast.

**Freshwater lake**: The only one on Crete is **Lake Kournás**, behind Georgioúpolis on the north coast, covering 65ha (160 acres).

## THE LAND

Subtly different from any other island in this region, Crete has a distinctive character shaped by its land-forms and position in the Mediterranean. Its elongated form lies across Latitude 35°, placing it further south than parts of the North African coastline and making it the most southerly point in Europe.

The largest of the Greek islands, Crete is 250km (155 miles) long and 60km (37 miles) across at its widest point, narrowing down to 12km (7.5 miles) across at the isthmus of Ierápetra in the east. Covering around 8400km² (3240 sq miles), it is the fifth largest island in the Mediterranean after Sicily, Sardinia, Corsica and Cyprus.

Dominated by four great mountain ranges, Crete would resemble a giant wedge if viewed in cross-section, with the thin end of the wedge to the north. The mountains slope down gradually from their lofty peaks to rolling foothills and broad coastal plains on the north side, where the island's major towns and cities – many established centuries ago – are strung out along a series of great bays. The north coast is still the most populous and densely developed part of the island. To the south the peaks drop precipitously to the sea, with small fishing villages huddled beneath the mighty cliffs and a

*During the spring Crete is ablaze with meadows of wild flowers against a backdrop of snow-clad peaks.*

sparse population dispersed along the rocky, windswept coast. Ierápetra is the only sizeable town on this side of the island.

## Mountains and High Plateaux

Crete's mountain ranges form an almost unbroken chain from one end of the island to the other. To the west, the **Lefká Óri (White Mountains)** present a formidable, craggy barrier, with peaks which are often still covered in snow in the early summer. The great height and steepness of their southern slopes has allowed mountain streams to etch deep gorges (such as **Samariá** and the **Ímbros Ravine**) through their limestone flanks. In the centre of the island the **Mount Ídha Massif** (also known as the **Psilorítis Range**) contains the island's highest summit and is often called 'the Roof of Crete'. To the east, the **Lasíthi Mountains** reach their highest points on Dhíkti at 2148m (7047ft) and its neighbour Aféndis Hristós at 2141m (7024ft). Beyond, the **Sitía Massif** seems almost to isolate the far eastern end of the island, although the peaks reach only a relatively modest 1476m (4842ft) at the top of Aféndis Kavoússi.

An unusual feature of Cretan geography is the number of high **plateaux** found tucked away in the higher elevations of the mountains. The biggest of these upland plains are the **Lasíthi Plateau**, the **Nídha Plateau** (beneath Psilorítis) and the **Omalós Plateau** (in the White Mountains). The gradual accumulation of soil washed down into these circular basins has turned them into fertile agricultural lands, well protected by the peaks which surround them. Travelling over barren mountain passes, it is a startling sight to be confronted with the contrast of the plateaux' green expanses at considerable altitudes.

**ANCIENT FOUNDATIONS**

Just 300km (190 miles) from the coast of Africa, Crete is at the southern boundary of the Aegean basin and geologically forms part of a large chain of islands stretching from mainland Greece through the Peloponnese and the Dodecanese to Turkey in the east. Thrust upwards during the Tertiary period Crete's mountains are mostly composed of crystalline limestone, schist and rocks which date back a further 140 million years to the Triassic period. The low-lying areas were formed well after the creation of the mountains, and consist of limestone, clays, sand and gypsum.

*The high Lasíthi plateau in eastern Crete is completely ringed by the Dhíkti Mountains.*

*Crown daisies bloom in profusion on the seafront near Haniá, with the Mediterranean sparkling invitingly beyond.*

## Climate

Crete's climate is typically Mediterranean although its southerly position means that the hot, dry summers last far longer here than they do elsewhere in Greece. There are no great regional variations between resorts at either end of the island, although the south coast is generally hotter than the north coast; you can rely on being able to swim on the north coast from April to September or October, and on the south coast until October or November.

**Spring** starts with the end of the winter rains in March, and wild flowers blossom all over the island during April and May. This is an excellent time to visit: there are few other tourists around, hoteliers are pleased to see you at the start of the season, and the days are warm and clear for exploring the countryside.

**Summer** gets into full swing by June, with temperatures and the crowds increasing throughout July and August. Although these are the hottest months and you may have to seek shade for much of the day, the humidity is low and the latter part of the day is delightful.

By **autumn** the island has dried out completely and dusty, lifeless landscapes predominate. Tourism slows down during September, the evenings are cooler, and the first sporadic rains send sunbathers scattering from the beaches. From October onwards the days are often mild and sunny, but rain becomes more regular, sometimes

### CRETAN WINDS

Summer temperatures on the north coast are often tempered by the cooling effects of the **meltémi**, which blows (sometimes for several days in a row) from the north/northwest. Whilst it has a beneficial effect in the north, by the time it zips up and over the mountains to the south coast it can reach 8 Beaufort or more. The south coast is also affected by the **sirocco**, blowing in off the Libyan Sahara. Not so benign in its consequences, the sirocco deposits sand and dust in every conceivable corner, slows down movement and leads to frayed tempers all round. It can last for days.

falling for days on end. The seas become rougher, with many of the summer excursion boats tied up in port.

During the **winter** most tourists have gone, hotels and tavernas close down and the rain sets in in earnest. Some visitors still head for the south coast, where **Ierápetra** enjoys the mildest climate on the island. Snowfalls mean that you can go skiing, although heavy snow often isolates remote mountain villages for weeks.

## Plant Life

Crete is exceptionally rich in plant life, despite the lack of native forests. This is mostly due to its climate and relative proximity to the tropics, where species diversity is far higher than in temperate regions. In fact, Crete boasts more than 1500 species of plants, around 130 of which are endemic to the island: most of these occur in the mountainous zones.

One of the most characteristic habitats, typically carpeted in wild flowers in spring, is the *phrígana*: this rocky, scrubby ground resembles the *garigue* found elsewhere in the Mediterranean and is often used for grazing goats and sheep. Beneath the low-growing (and usually thorny) bushes aromatic herbs such as sage, rosemary, thyme and oregano thrive, interspersed with flowering plants such as tassel hyacinths, irises, birthworts, fritillaries and the lovely Cretan ebony (*Ebenus cretica*). Orchids do well in the *phrígana*, with half a dozen or more species (including the endemic Cretan *Ophrys*) providing vivid splashes of colour in springtime.

Orchids are also often found on grazed areas behind beaches, with other **coastal regions** displaying the brilliant yellow horned poppy or the jewel-like pink campion (*Silene colorata*). Autumn-flowering plants include the tall, white-flowered sea squill, sea daffodils and autumn crocuses.

Between March and June **meadows** and **orchards** are transformed into a blaze of colour by tulips, poppies, flaxes, blue and purple vetches, chrysanthemums and wild gladioli.

The **mountains** are home to some of Crete's rarest

*Thanks to its southerly position near the coast of Africa, Crete is rich in plant life such as the pungent Dragon Arum, found on the Akrotíri peninsula.*

**WILD GOATS**

The most unusual animal on the island is the Cretan ibex or wild goat (*Capra aegagrus cretensis*), known locally as the *kri-kri*. This magnificent beast, with its large, wide-curling horns, is almost impossible to see in the wild, since it survives only in very limited numbers (mostly in the more inaccessible regions of the Lefká Óri) and grazes at night. Often depicted in Minoan art but hunted almost to extinction in the succeeding centuries, the preservation of the wild goat now depends on small colonies living on nature reserves on several of the uninhabited islands off the north coast.

species, but more familiar plants such as alyssums, aubretias and saxifrages flower in rocky areas in the late spring and early summer. Cyclamen, violets, pinks and gentians can be found in shady gorges, alongside several species of orchid. Higher up, various crocus species (including the lovely *Crocus sieberi*) appear as soon as the snow melts in the spring.

## Animals and Birds

Apart from the ubiquitous sheep, goats, donkeys and other domestic animals, Crete has little in the way of animal life. Exceptions include wild goats and the equally elusive Cretan spiny mouse. There are several species of snake (none of which is harmful) and frogs. Crete is one of the few places in Europe, and the only location in Greece, where you might see a chameleon. Loggerhead turtles breed on beaches to the west of Haniá and around Mátala and Réthimnon.

Basking on rocks or on a sunny wall you might see a small local lizard known as Erhard's wall lizard, whereas a bright green flash in the scrubby bushes of the *phrígana* is more likely to be the Balkan green lizard. Geckos

*A familiar sight all over the island: a nanny goat tethered in an olive grove.*

*Butterflies are the most spectacular insects of the Cretan spring and summer, and include this large swallowtail, bright yellow Cleopatras and the small green hairstreaks.*

perform a useful service picking off the mosquitoes and other insects inside your room, so don't shoo them away if you happen to see them clinging to your ceiling – a feat they're able to perform due to the round adhesive pads on each toe.

The lack of wildlife on the ground is more than compensated for by the surprising variety of **birds** on the island. Crete is an ideal place for watching migratory species which spend the winter in Africa and stop off in the eastern Mediterranean on the way to their summer breeding grounds in northern Europe between March and May. The return migration takes place in the autumn.

The **mountains** are one of the best places for rare and interesting species, as well as alpine chough, alpine accentor, blue rock thrush, alpine swifts, crag martins and spectacled warblers. Rocky crags provide nesting sites for dramatic **birds of prey** such as peregrine, golden and Bonelli's eagle and vultures – the latter include the griffon vulture and the rare lammergeier which has a wingspan of up to 3m (10ft).

Further down, the **hillsides** are good places to look for buntings, the chukar (a relative of the red-legged partridge) and the spectacular golden oriole. In the **coastal zones** you may spot Sardinian and Rüppell's warblers, cirl buntings and even Eleonora's falcons. Yellow-legged herring gulls are common around harbour areas.

---

### MARSH BIRDS

Being such a dry island, Crete has few major wetland habitats but there are several small pockets of marshland and estuarine areas which are good places to look for migratory birds in the spring and early summer. Waders such as herons, egrets, ringed plovers, avocet and black-winged stilt can often be seen in these areas, and marsh harriers are fairly common. Most of the wetland habitats are on the north coast, in particular around **Lake Kournás**, the estuary at **Georgioúpolis** and behind the beach at **Almirós** near **Áyios Nikólaos**.

## THE DATING GAME

The man who discovered Knossós and put flesh on the bones of what had previously been only myth was **Sir Arthur Evans** (see pages 46–7) and it was he who named this great culture 'Minoan' after the legendary King Minos. Evans also devised a dating system to help identify the different periods in Minoan history, but this becomes so complicated (with subdivisions based on different pottery styles) that it is confusing to anyone but an archaeologist. His basic divisions were **Early Minoan** (EM), **Middle Minoan** (MM) and **Late Minoan** (LM). A simplified chronology would read:

- **Prepalatial Period** (3000–1900 BC); EMI–MMI in the Evans system.
- **First Palace Period** (1900–1700 BC); MMI–MMII (Evans), also known as the 'Old Palace' or 'Protopalatial Period'.
- **New Palace Period** (1700–1450 BC); MMIII–LMI (Evans), also called the 'Neopalatial Period'.
- **Postpalatial Period** (1450–1100 BC); LMII–LMIII (Evans).

## HISTORY IN BRIEF

The first settlers to arrive on Crete came here around 6000 BC, probably from Asia Minor or Africa. They brought with them the rudiments of Stone Age culture, making basic tools and crude pottery, and led a semi-nomadic existence, mostly living in caves. Gradually they started to practise agriculture, build houses and create more refined pottery – including small figurines of animals and humans and idols of a fertility goddess. The earliest settlements were in central and eastern Crete, but over the centuries they eventually spread throughout the island.

### THE BRONZE AGE
#### Prepalatial Period (3000–1900 BC)

Between 3000 and 2500 BC significant changes began to occur on Crete which can only have been caused by a fresh wave of immigrants arriving from Asia Minor, where great civilizations already existed. Copper-working was brought to the island, along with weaving and more sophisticated ceramic techniques. Towns and villages sprang up and prospered, and the first tombs were built. The olive and the vine were introduced, and mercantile trade opened up routes to other countries.

These developments led to the rise of what we now call **Minoan civilization**. Over the next 1200 years this society built magnificent palaces and (partly thanks to Crete's strategic position at the crossroads between east

*The Throne Room of the Palace of Knossós, lined with benches on either side of the stone throne and decorated with a fresco of griffins.*

## HISTORICAL CALENDAR

**6000 BC** Earliest inhabitants arrive on Crete, living in caves and making crude tools and pottery.
**3000–1900 BC** Prepalatial Period. Beginning of Minoan civilization.
**1900–1700 BC** First Palace Period. Palaces built at Knossós, Phaistós and Mália. Development of Linear A script.
**1700 BC** Earthquake destroys first palaces.
**1700–1450 BC** New Palace Period. Flowering of Minoan civilization and building of great palaces of Knossós, Phaistós, Mália and Zákros. Development of Linear B.
**1500 BC** Eruption of Santorini.
**1450 BC** Destruction of new palaces. Invasion by Mycenaeans.
**1450–1100 BC** Postpalatial Period.
**1100 BC** Invasion by Dorians. Final decline of Minoan civilization.
**69 BC** Invasion by Romans. Crete becomes part of Roman province ruled from Górtyn.
**AD 59** St Paul introduces Christianity. Titus becomes first bishop of Crete.
**AD 395** Roman Empire splits: Crete becomes part of Byzantine Empire.
**AD 824** Arab conquest.
**AD 961** Liberation from Arab rule.
**1204** Fourth Crusade sacks Constantinople: end of Byzantine Empire, Crete sold to Venice.
**1645** Invasion by Turks.
**1669** Iráklion conquered by Turks.
**1770** Revolt under Dhaskaloyiánnis.
**1821** Greek War of Independence breaks out.
**1832** Greek Independence; Crete ruled by Egypt before reverting to the Turks.
**1866** Explosion at Moní Arkádhi.
**1897** Occupation by Great Powers.
**1898** Independence.
**1908** Cretan Assembly declares *Énosis*.
**1913** Union with Greece.
**1941** Battle of Crete; German occupation.
**1945** Liberation.
**1960** Beginning of tourist boom.

and west) established dominion over much of the eastern Mediterranean. It was the first truly great European civilization, and its highly developed culture still exerts a fascinating pull today.

### First Palace Period (1900–1700 BC)

Minoan society developed a structured class system, with rigid hierarchies and a slave class. It was probably slaves who built the first of the great palaces at **Knossós**, **Phaistós** and **Mália**. The Minoans strengthened their rule over the region and the security and prosperity of the island led to the growth of large towns around the palaces.

Important advances were made in the development of **pottery**, with the delicate **Kamáres ware** now being produced on potters' wheels. Tools, daggers and other weapons were elaborately cast and **jewellery** became a fine art, with delicate filigree techniques and decorative patterns adorning some of the fabulous pieces from this era. **Seals** (used extensively in trading) became more sophisticated.

### THE MYSTERY SCRIPT

Towards the end of the First Palace Period the Minoans developed a syllable-based script, now known as **Linear A**, to write down their language. Although it seems to have been mostly used to keep administrative records (such as the palace accounts) on baked clay tablets, it has also been found on pottery, libation tables and jewellery. Linear A has never been successfully deciphered but its successor, **Linear B** (developed during the New Palace Period) was cracked by an Englishman, Michael Ventris, in 1953. Unfortunately, Linear B texts tell us little about Minoan life apart from the fact that they liked to keep lists and inventories.

*Ceremonial drinking vessel, or* rhyton, *in the form of a bull's head, from the Palace of Knossós.*

Religious life became more central to Minoan society, with the development of the **peak sanctuaries**. The dead began to be buried in large clay vessels (known as *pithoi*) and sarcophagi.

All the first palaces, as well as the towns, were completely destroyed, probably by a massive **earthquake**, around 1700 BC.

## The New Palace Period (1700–1450 BC)

Despite the devastation, the Minoans rebuilt their palaces – this time on an even grander scale than before. The new palaces were elaborate architectural constructions on several floors with grand stairways inside the buildings, efficient plumbing systems, colonnaded porticoes and courtyards, workshops for artisans and large theatral areas outside for ritual performances. The walls were decorated with finely painted frescoes and large areas were set aside to house numerous, huge storage jars, testimony to the wealth of the inhabitants.

Outside the palaces the towns and country villas were rebuilt and trade prospered. The Minoans had close allies and even some colonies elsewhere in the Mediterranean, and they apparently lived with no fear of attack from outside or even from within: none of the ruins show any signs at all of defences having been built. Historians interpret this as a sign that the Minoans relied heavily on seapower as a means of defence, in addition to the support of their trading colonies throughout the Cyclades.

The palaces were the central focus of religious life, with the famous bull-leaping contests probably taking place in their theatral areas.

This was also the golden age of artistic expression, most notably in the vivid, lifelike frescoes which adorned the palace walls. Craftsmen excelled in stonework, gold jewellery and highly decorative pottery. Sculpted figures of animals, deities and humans were also common. Sealstone work became even more elaborate and brilliant.

## Decline and Fall

Two hundred and fifty years after the New Palaces had been built they were again destroyed in a wide-ranging catastrophe. Controversy still rages over the causes of this devastation, one theory suggesting that it was linked to the eruption of the volcanic island of Santorini, 150km (93 miles) to the north.

However, the Santorini eruption has now been more precisely dated and seems to have occurred fifty years *before* the destruction on Crete. Some archaeologists now believe that the Minoan civilization was in fact destroyed by outside invaders, most probably the Mycenaeans. This theory is supported by the emergence of the **Linear B** script (an early form of Greek) before the end of the New Palace period, suggesting that the Mycenaeans were already dominating the Minoans. Why they should want to destroy palaces which they already controlled is a mystery which still remains to be solved.

### KING MINOS

Sir Arthur Evans named the ancient civilization which he had unearthed after the legendary King Minos, but in fact it turns out that there were no less than 22 rulers called Minos – the name simply means 'priest-king', a label similar to that given to the dynasty of Pharoahs in Egypt.

*Large storage jars like this, known as* pithoi, *were used by the Minoans for storing oil and wine.*

### The Postpalatial Period (1450–1100 BC)

The Mycenaeans were now firmly in control of Crete, rebuilding Knossós (which had suffered less than the other palaces in the devastation) and administering the island from there. Some former palaces (such as at Gourniá, Ayía Triádha and Tílissos) were re-occupied, but the others were left in ruins. The city of **Kydonia** (beneath present-day Haniá) flourished, but elsewhere coastal settlements were abandoned and the inhabitants moved inland. Minoan art still flourished, particularly in the design of *larnakes* (sarcophagi).

Descending from the Balkans, the **Dorians** began to overrun the Mycenaeans in mainland Greece and by 1100 BC they had arrived in Crete, eclipsing the last remnants of the island's once-great civilization.

### THE EVERGREEN TREE

Zeus and Europa consummated their union at **Górtyn**, beneath the shady canopy of a spreading plane tree which Zeus had brought down specially from the mountains. The tree became everlasting and evergreen, never shedding its leaves in winter. It is said still to exist: follow the path at Górtyn alongside the river behind the Odeon (see page 59) inside the site and you'll see the ancient tree there, marked by a plaque in Greek.

*This flask from Palékastro, now in the Iráklion Museum, dates from the 15th century BC. The octopus motif is typical of Minoan decoration of the period.*

## MYTHOLOGY

Crete played a crucial role in ancient Greek legends. This was largely due to the belief that **Zeus** was born and brought up here; Zeus was central to the creation of the Greek pantheon and his beginnings form the cornerstone of Greek mythology. Zeus' son **Minos** was another significant figure in the chronicles of the Greek gods.

### Father of the Gods

In the beginning **Gaia**, or Mother Earth, gave birth to Uranus (the Sky), Pontos (the Sea) and Ourea (the Mountains). Gaia married Uranus – who became ruler of the world – and produced the Titans, the youngest of whom was **Kronos**. Kronos overthrew Uranus and married his own sister, **Rhea**, with whom he produced many children. Fearful that he would suffer the same fate as his own father, Kronos ate all five of his children.

When Rhea discovered this she hid her next son, **Zeus**, and fooled Kronos by giving him a stone wrapped in swaddling to eat instead. Zeus was secretly brought up in the **Dhiktean Cave** (see page 71). On reaching manhood he tricked Kronos into vomiting up his siblings (being gods, they had remained alive in his stomach) with whom he formed an alliance to fight Kronos and the Titans. After a decade of battles, Zeus became the undisputed ruler of the gods – reigning from Mount Olympus – and Kronos was banished to the underworld.

One day Zeus spied the beautiful princess **Europa** picking flowers on a distant shore. He appeared to her in the form of a bull and carried her off on his back across the sea to Crete, landing at Mátala and then travelling to Górtyn, where he ravished her under a plane tree. Europa gave birth to three sons, Sarpedon, Rhadamanthys and **Minos**.

## Minos and the Minotaur

Europa married Asterios, king of Crete, who adopted her three sons. On his death, Minos and Sarpedon vied for the throne. Minos called on Poseidon for help, demanding a white **bull** which would rise up from the waves as proof of his divinity. He promised Poseidon that he would then sacrifice the bull but when it appeared – confirming Minos' claim to the throne – it was so beautiful that Minos hid it amongst his herds. As punishment, Poseidon caused Minos' wife **Pasiphaë** to fall in love with the bull and their coupling resulted in the birth of the **Minotaur**, a human with a bull's head. Enraged, Minos ordered the inventor **Daedalos** to build a labyrinth in which he imprisoned the Minotaur.

Meanwhile, Minos was engaged in a war with Athens, which he won. As a penalty, he demanded that the Athenians send an annual tribute of seven youths and seven maidens to sacrifice to the Minotaur. **Theseus**, son of the Athenian king, decided that this subjugation must stop and set out on the third voyage among the sacrificial victims. **Ariadne**, Minos' daughter, fell in love with Theseus when he arrived in Crete and plotted to help him kill the Minotaur. On Daedalos' advice she gave him a ball of thread to help find his way out of the maze once the deed was done. The plan worked and the couple fled the island.

When Minos discovered this treachery he ordered Daedalos and his son **Icarus** to be thrown into the labyrinth. They escaped by making wings of feathers held together with wax and, although Daedalos reached Sicily safely, Icarus flew too close to the sun, melting the wax of his wings and falling to his death in the sea.

Minos met his end while pursuing Daedalos and was banished to the underworld.

---

### THE MINOTAUR AT KNOSSÓS

According to legend, Daedalos' labyrinth, which he built to imprison the Minotaur, was at Knossós. It was a massive building with numerous rooms, false passages and hidden corners. Could this be the Palace of Knossós itself, with King Minos keeping his citizens subjugated by the threat of the Minotaur inside?

*One of the magnificent frescoes from the Palace of Knossós, painted in the 16th century BC, this elegant young man crowned with feathers was identified by Arthur Evans as the 'priest-king'.*

*Opposite: The apse is all that now survives of the 6th-century church of Áyios Títos at Górtyn, once an important centre of early Christianity on the island.*

## CRETE UNDER FOREIGN RULE
### The Iron Age to Byzantium

As the Dorians spread throughout Crete some of the original inhabitants retreated to mountain settlements; they became known as **Eteocretans**, or 'true Cretans', and still adhered to some Minoan traditions. The Dorians brought iron tools to replace bronze, and were almost constantly at war with each other. Little progress was made and Crete sank into obscurity as a mere province under Athenian rule. The only significant achievement during this period was the famous **Law Code of Górtyn** (see page 59) which was the first body of written law in ancient Europe.

By the middle of the 2nd century BC most of Greece had fallen under Roman rule. The Romans mounted an unsuccessful expedition against Crete in 71 BC and two years later invaded again under **Quintus Metellus**, but it was a further three years before the island was completely subjugated. Crete became part of a Roman province which included Cyrenaica in North Africa, and **Górtyn** was built up into a powerful capital.

Several centuries of peace and prosperity followed, with the Romans building a network of roads, irrigation systems and aqueducts. **Christianity** arrived when St Paul landed on the south coast in AD 59, bringing with him **Titus** who became Crete's first bishop.

With the division of the Roman Empire in AD 395, Crete became part of the eastern **Byzantine Empire** under the rule of the new imperial capital of Constantinople (now Istanbul). Christianity continued to flourish, with some 70 churches being built on the island – the best preserved of which is the basilica of **Áyios Títos** at Górtyn.

### The Arab Conquest

The disintegration of the Roman Empire from the 7th century onwards led to upheavals throughout the Mediterranean, and by AD 824 Crete had fallen prey to a band of **Arab** adventurers. All the great cities and churches were sacked, and for over a hundred years the

*Below: Having conquered Crete, the Romans made their capital at Górtyn; this is one of many statues unearthed in the former city.*

island became little more than a pirate base from which the conquerors attacked ships and nearby islands.

## The Second Byzantine Period

Crete was eventually recaptured from the Arabs by the Byzantine general **Nikefóras Fokás**, and many settlers were brought to the island from Constantinople and mainland Greece. Prosperity gradually returned, and 12 noble families were brought to the colony to strengthen Byzantine rule – their descendants remained influential right into the Middle Ages.

## The Venetian Period

In 1204 the **Fourth Crusade** attacked Constantinople, bringing about the end of the Byzantine Empire. Crete was sold to the **Venetians** for a nominal sum, but before they could take control the rival **Genoese** established themselves on the island. It was another five years before the Venetians could oust them.

Under the Venetians, Crete was mercilessly exploited for its timber and agricultural resources, with the population heavily taxed and kept under strict subjugation. Orthodox churches were seized and high-ranking priests expelled from the island. Over the next 150 years there were no less than ten rebellions against Venetian rule; the Venetians built a series of forts and defences around the major towns, in fear as much of the local populace as of foreign invaders.

### A GRUESOME SIEGE

The Arab conquerors built a massive fortress at what was then known as Heraclium (the present-day capital of Iráklion) which they called **Rabdh el Khandak** or 'the castle of the ditch', referring to the huge moat which surrounded it. When the Byzantine forces landed in 961 they ambushed a large Arab contingent which had been sent to reinforce Rabdh el Khandak, cut off their heads and arranged thousands of them in two circles around the outside of the moat – hundreds more were catapulted over the walls into the fort. The demoralized Arab forces soon capitulated to the Byzantine general.

### FRESCOED CHURCHES

Under the Venetians, Roman Catholicism became the official religion and around 380 monasteries were built on the island. But the Orthodox faith was strongly rooted amongst the local populace and they continued to build small churches and chapels, decorating them with Byzantine frescoes. It's estimated that there were once more than 800 frescoed churches in Crete, most of them built in the 14th and 15th centuries, and that at least 600 of these have partially survived.

More streets and squares are named after **Eleftherios Venizélos** than any other Cretan. Born near Haniá in 1864, as a young man he had fought in rebellions against the Turks and became a key member of the Cretan Assembly. In 1905 he forced the resignation of the regent appointed by the Great Powers, and in 1908 the Assembly unilaterally declared *Énosis* (union with Greece). Amidst political turmoil Venizélos was elected Prime Minister of Greece – the first of his many tenures of this office. He was an influential figure in Greek politics until 1935, and on his death in 1936 was buried on the Akrotiri Peninsula near Haniá (see pages 106–7).

## The Turkish Occupation

From the 15th century onwards the **Turks** had been challenging Venetian dominance of the eastern Mediterranean, and it did not take the Ottoman armies long to capture the island when they eventually attacked in 1645. Only **Iráklion** held out, withstanding a long and bitter siege for 21 years.

Over the next two centuries Cretans suffered heavy taxes and exploitation under Turkish rule. There were forcible conversions of whole villages to Islam, although many people continued to worship as Christians in secret. Others fled to the mountains, from where they launched frequent revolts – the first of which was led by **Ioánnis Dhaskaloyiánnis** in 1770. In 1821 the **War of Greek Independence** was launched, but it was ruthlessly crushed with the help of Egyptian troops.

*Overlooking the beautiful harbour at Haniá, the Mosque of the Janissaries is the oldest Ottoman building on the island. It was erected in 1645, at the beginning of the Turkish occupation.*

Although the European powers intervened their actions lacked teeth and whilst Greece became an independent state in 1832, Crete was left in the hands of the Egyptians and then handed back to the Turks.

The final straw came in 1898 when 17 British troops were killed in Iráklion and the Great Powers insisted on Turkish withdrawal.

## Union with Greece

Although Crete was now autonomous, most Cretans wanted union with the mainland. **Elefthérios Venizélos** emerged as their leader, staging a coup in 1905. After he had become Premier of Greece Venizélos engineered the **Union with Greece** which took place on 30 May 1913.

## World War II and After

As the Germans overran the Greek mainland in 1941 the Greek government, the army and most of the Allied forces that had been sent to Greece withdrew to Crete. On 21 May the German invasion began. Although they suffered heavy losses they managed to secure the airstrip at Máleme, and poured in troops and equipment in such quantity that the Allies were routed. The **Battle of Crete** was over in just a week and the Allies fled to the south coast where most were taken off by boat.

Throughout the war Cretans put up fierce resistance to the German occupation, and heroically helped the troops left behind to escape. Terrible retribution followed the Cretans' guerrilla actions, with whole villages wiped out. When the Germans finally withdrew in 1945 they left behind an island in tatters, with a shattered economy, depopulated villages and burned-out cities.

Crete rapidly rebuilt its economy, founded on agriculture and later tourism. Politics remained dominated by the age-old Cretan distrust of outsiders – including control by Athens. This has been assuaged somewhat by recent government reforms, but hostility is still directed at NATO, which maintains several large bases on the island.

### THE CAPTURE OF GENERAL KREIPE

One of the most audacious acts of the Cretan resistance was the kidnapping of General Kreipe, the German commander, in 1944. From where he was snatched outside Iráklion he was smuggled right across the island past 22 German roadblocks and taken off by submarine to Egypt. One of the British intelligence officers who helped in the operation was Stanley Moss, whose book *Ill Met by Moonlight* (available locally in several languages) describes this daring coup. Needless to say, swift retribution followed the kidnapping.

## THE REGIONS

Crete is divided into four administrative areas, known as *nome*:
- **Haniá**: population 133,060. Capital Haniá, population 65,519.
- **Réthimnon**: population 69,260. Capital Réthimnon, population 23,595.
- **Iráklion**: population 263,868. Capital Iráklion, population 127,600.
- **Lasíthi**: population 70,769. Capital Ayios Nikólaos, population 8500.

# GOVERNMENT AND ECONOMY

Crete is one of ten administrative districts of Greece, and sends 15 members to the Athens parliament. Politically, the Cretans' attitude is shaped by their long history of fighting for independence and they remain resentful of outside control – including government from Athens.

Until recently, the appointment of prefecture governors was determined in Athens, but with the local government reforms introduced at the time of the 1994 local elections (which affected the whole of Greece) there is now a far greater degree of decentralization and local control. Since taking up office at the beginning of 1995, members elected to the self-governing prefectures have been gradually taking over responsibility for matters such as roads, schools, hospitals and economic development of the regions. Defence, foreign affairs and law and order remain the responsibility of central government.

Crete attracts significant aid from EU funds, and it is noticeable as you drive round the island how many new road projects are bankrolled by the EU.

### Agriculture

Crete has few natural resources and minimal industry. A large proportion of its inhabitants still depend on small-scale agriculture and animal husbandry, rearing goats, sheep, pigs and poultry. **Vines** and **olives** play an important role in the rural economy, and it is estimated that almost half the island is **pasture** for the hundreds and thousands of goats and sheep kept here.

Crete's climate is extremely beneficial for the growing of **fruit**, in particular citrus fruits, figs, almonds, apricots, quince, pomegranate and carob.

In many parts of the country, and especially on the warmer south coast, you will see hundreds of **polytunnels** (plastic greenhouses) spread over the land. These were introduced to the island by a Dutchman, Paul Kuipers, in the 1960s and, although most visitors lament their unsightly presence, they have proved an enormous boon to the Cretans. Polytunnels have

*Native of Central Asia, the pomegranate thrives in the sunny Mediterranean climate.*

*Wherever you go in Crete you are likely to come across flocks of sheep ambling along the country roads.*

significantly extended the growing season for crops such as tomatoes, cucumbers and melons, and enabled new crops such as bananas, avocados, kiwi fruit and pineapples to be grown. Crete is now a major exporter of fruit and vegetables, in particular supplying the Athens markets in the winter months.

## Tourism

Tourism now forms one of the mainstays of the Cretan economy. The first tourists to arrive here at the beginning of the century were purely interested in the Minoan heritage, and these earnest travellers probably saw little else of the island at all.

Mass tourism began in the 1960s, with the construction of numerous hotels along the north coast – which had the best beaches and easiest access from ports and airports. Much of this development, and the building boom which has followed since, has been badly planned, turning many areas of the north coast into an ugly mess of hotels, apartment complexes and beach resorts.

Today, most tourists (around 2 million annually) arrive on charter packages, but investment in infrastructure has not kept pace with this growth – Iráklion airport, for instance, remains grossly inadequate despite recent improvements.

---

**COINING IT FROM THE MINOANS**

The six main historical sites on Crete (including Iráklion Museum) are visited by a total of around 1.5 million people, generating approximately 1400 million drachmas (about £2.7 million) in entrance fees annually. The three most popular sites are:

- **Knossós**: 685,000 visitors annually, with a peak of around 130,000 in the month of August (about 4200 per day).
- **Iráklion Museum**: 400,000 visitors a year (2,300 a day in August).
- **Phaistós**: 145,000 visitors a year (800 per day in August).

It's clear that if sightseeing rather than sunbathing is your main interest, August is a month to avoid!

---

**FOREIGN ARRIVALS**

Crete is most popular with the **Germans** (who account for around 609,143 tourists every year), followed by the **British** (254,124), the **Scandinavians** (387,137) and the **Dutch** (145,083).

**DOING THE 'VOLTA'**

One aspect of traditional Cretan society which has changed very little is the ritual of the *vólta*, an evening stroll in which whole families (or groups of young men and women) parade back and forth around the village square, on the seafront, or up and down a particular street. It's a chance to wear one's best clothes (particularly at weekends) and socialize with friends and neighbours, and it has always been the village marriage market, with prospective partners able to check each other out under parental supervision.

*An Iráklion portrait photographer awaits his next subject.*

## THE PEOPLE

The Cretans are a proud people whose character has been shaped by the island's long and often bitter struggle against foreign invaders. They are also renowned for their friendliness and **hospitality**, although nowadays these qualities are often stretched to breaking-point in the face of an overwhelming onslaught by the most recent invaders, arriving by the plane-load for their holidays (in peak months there are nearly as many foreigners on the island as there are Cretans). The ancient custom of *philoxenía*, a duty of hospitality to strangers, has all but disappeared, surviving in many places as nothing more than an inviting name for a guesthouse.

**Tourism** has inevitably brought changes to the traditional way of life, some of them positive (such as increased prosperity), others less desirable (such as increasing urbanization and the desertion of rural villages as young people flock to the tourist honeypots to earn money). Despite this, the four main regions in Crete still retain their individual cultural identities, with their own customs and dialects.

The **family** remains the cornerstone of the Cretan community, in particular the 'extended family' consisting of a nucleus of at least three generations, presided over by the father as the central authority. Sometimes all three generations may live in the same house, with newly-weds moving into the home of the bridegroom's father. Amongst other things, the extended family functions as an economic safety net should close relatives need help of any sort.

The most important family celebrations are **christenings** and **weddings**, with the latter often involving whole villages in huge marriage feasts.

# RELIGION

The **Orthodox Church** plays an important role in everyday Cretan life. Under the overall jurisdiction of the Patriarch of Istanbul, the Orthodox Church is ruled by an Archbishop (based in Iráklion) and four bishops (one in each of the four regions). Beneath them are the *papádes*, or parish priests, who officiate at baptisms, weddings and funerals. Saints' day festivals (or *paniyíria*) are an important part of the religious calendar.

The continuing support for Orthodoxy on Crete can be partly attributed to the fact that the church displayed a steely will in keeping the flames of Christianity alive during the long repression under the Turks, and the monasteries continued their role as bastions of resistance against invaders during World War II, when they sheltered and aided Allied troops and their Cretan counterparts. The church has also been crucial in defending and perpetuating the Greek **language** and **culture** over the centuries.

## BLOOD FEUDS

In the past, the Cretans' fierce pride and sense of family honour often led to vendettas between families which could continue for years, in an escalating cycle of retribution as each side sought to avenge the violence against them. The last recorded feud of this type took place in the 1940s in the remote and mountainous **Sfakiá** region, where the people have always had a reputation for lawlessness. It lasted nine years and is said to have claimed 20 lives.

## MINIATURE MEMORIALS

All over Crete you'll notice small memorials on the roadsides, usually a simple, miniature replica of a church or chapel, but often hugely elaborate affairs with fanciful embellishments and decoration. Known as **iconostasia**, these memorials often contain an oil lamp or an icon and are a reminder of an important event (such as a fatal crash) which took place on that spot. On mountainous hair-pin bends you'll often see several together, a useful warning that it's an accident black spot.

*These little wayside shrines are a common sight as you tour around the island.*

### EASTER IN CRETE

Easter in Crete is a joyous, unforgettable event and some holiday companies even operate special trips to coincide with it. Note, however, that it is observed in accordance with the Orthodox calendar, which means that it can be anything from one to four weeks ahead of the Roman calendar. Also, flights and ferries to Crete are very heavily booked at this time, as people return home to celebrate, so check availability well in advance.

## TRADITIONAL CULTURE

Most of the more colourful, traditional Cretan **costumes** are now rarely worn and are usually seen only in the display cases of museums. Up in the mountains you might well see old men in the villages wearing traditional baggy black breeches – known as *wráka*, they have been around since the 16th century – tucked into high boots, with the *saríki*, a black-fringed scarf, wrapped around their heads. It is rarer to see women sporting their traditional, elaborately decorated costumes (except in staged performances).

**Music** and **dance** are as important as they are elsewhere in Greece, although the Cretan style is more unpredictable and wild. The main instruments are the **lyre** (brought over by the Venetians), accompanied by the **lute** and the **tambouras**. The traditional Cretan flute (*askomantoura*) is sometimes still played in remote rural areas.

The most popular **songs** are the *mantinathes*, which are spirited, rhyming couplets with everyone joining in for the chorus. Although there are *mantinathes* for every occasion many are created on the spot, with plenty of relevant jokes thrown in! The oldest songs are the *risitika* ballads, created in the Lefká Óri (White Mountains) many centuries ago. These ballads recount heroic deeds and express the desire for freedom.

The best-known Cretan dance is the *pentozalis*, a five-step which originated in eastern Crete: the dancers hold onto each other in a line and follow the leader's steps, with the pace rapidly quickening and the lead dancer breaking off to perform acrobatic jumps as the music reaches a crescendo. The *sirtos*, found all over Greece, is a fast round dance which has many local variations on Crete. The only dance performed by couples is the *sousta*, which was introduced by the Venetians.

*A fishing boat, with traditional tackle, hauled up on the beach at Plataniás, west of Haniá. Fishing remains an important acitivity in many coastal areas.*

*Music and dance are intimately woven into the fabric of Cretan life.*

## FESTIVALS

The most important festival in the Greek (and Cretan) calendar is **Easter**, which is celebrated with considerable fervour. Although fasting isn't nowadays strictly observed during Lent, once Holy Week comes round all television and radio programmes take on a religious theme and services are held everywhere. On **Good Friday** people queue up to pay homage to the *Epitáphion*, the Christ figure laid out for burial, and that night the funeral bier is paraded through the streets with a huge procession following it.

On Easter Saturday night Christ's return is celebrated with a mass which starts on the stroke of midnight: an atmospheric, candlelit service with the congregation chanting *'Hristós anésti'* ('He is risen'). Afterwards, fireworks light up the sky as the church bells toll (it used to be guns, until they were banned after some accidental deaths).

The Lenten fast is broken on **Easter Sunday** with a soup of lamb's offal (*mayirítsa*) and then the lamb itself is roasted, with the heady scent of garlic, oil and herbs wafting through every village as the meat turns on the spits. Music and dancing follow.

As well as the main festivals there are numerous smaller ones held in honour of the patron saints of the village churches on their name-days.

### FESTIVAL CALENDAR

**6–7 Jan**: Feast of the Epiphany, with blessing of baptismal fonts and open water (including the sea) everywhere.
**Lent**: Carnival processions, masquerades and celebrations.
**25 Mar**: Independence Day, parades and dancing to commemorate the 1821 uprising.
**1 May**: May Day, with garlands of flowers on every door to celebrate the spring.
**20–27 May**: Anniversary of the Battle of Crete.
**24 June**: Birth of John the Baptist, marked by the lighting of midsummer bonfires.
**July**: Week-long wine festival in Réthimnon.
**15 Aug**: Assumption of the Virgin, extensively celebrated.
**Mid–Aug:** Sitia Sultana Festival.
**25 Aug**: Festival of St Titus, Crete's patron saint, with large processions in Iráklion.
**29–30 Aug**: Two-day festival on the Rodhópou Peninsula in honour of John the Baptist.
**Mid-Oct**: Chestnut festival in the south-west.
**28 Oct**: 'Óhi Day': a national holiday celebrating the one-word Greek reply ('Óhi', meaning 'No') to Mussolini's ultimatum to capitulate in 1940.
**7–9 Nov**: National holiday celebrating the explosion at the Arkádhi Monastery in 1866 (see page 89).

*Octopuses drying in the sun: the chopped-up tentacles may be grilled over charcoal and served as an appetizer.*

## FOOD AND DRINK

Greece is not renowned for gourmet food but at its best a meal on Crete can be a delight: sitting at an outdoor table with the sea sparkling beyond, with a chilled bottle of *retsína*, a fresh Greek salad and chargrilled *souvláki* before you, the cares of the world seem a long way away.

The most common type of restaurant is the **taverna**, where you'll find a range of baked dishes (see below) as well as grills, fish and salads. A **psistariá** is a restaurant specializing in spit roasts (such as lamb with herbs) and grills: if there is one nearby it's always worth checking out. A **psarótaverna** specializes in fish dishes.

Although you'll be handed a menu on arrival (usually in Greek and English), it's often a dog-eared, printed form which gives little indication of what is actually available that day. In a typical taverna there is usually a display counter where you can see what's on offer, be it cuts of meat and fish or pre-prepared dishes. In smaller, traditional tavernas you can also ask to have a look in the kitchen and make your choice from the simmering pots and prepared dishes there.

Unless you specify otherwise, all the dishes you've ordered will come at once, except for Greek salad which is usually served as a starter. Set menus are something of a rarity – you simply order whatever combination you want from the menu.

The best-known Greek starter is the *meze*, a selection of small titbits such as slices of tomato, cucumber and melon, chunks of cheese, mussels, olives and other bite-sized nibbles. Other appetizers include *taramósalata* (made with smoked and puréed cod's roe), *tsatsíki* (yoghurt and cucumber dip with garlic), *melitzanosaláta* (aubergine dip) and *dolmádhes* (stuffed vine leaves).

*Four friends settling down to a game of* távli, *or backgammon. This is a familiar sight in many a Cretan village* kafeníon, *still largely a male preserve.*

The most common local meat is *lamb*, but *pork*, *beef* and *goat* are also available. *Souvláki* is chunks of meat (lamb or pork) sprinkled with oregano and grilled over charcoal on a skewer; it's available everywhere, including fast food outlets, and is usually very reasonably priced. *Paidákia* is chargrilled lamb chops, at their best when lean and tender. Chicken (*kotópoulo*) is a common standby. One of the best dishes is *stifádo*, a stew with beef, tomatoes and onions, traditionally cooked in a clay pot.

Often the best value meals are the various baked dishes, the best known of which is *moussaká* (mince, aubergines and potatoes topped with a béchamel sauce); others include *pastítsio* (noodles, meat and tomatoes baked with cheese) and *kleftikó* (a local speciality of meat, potatoes and vegetables cooked in a clay pot).

Overfishing around Cretan waters means that fish is now incredibly expensive, although quite delicious if you can afford it. It's normally sold by weight, once you have selected your fish from the chiller. Red mullet (*barbóunia*), swordfish (*ksifías*), octopus (*ktapódi*) and squid (*kalamári*) are all available – at a price. The cheapest fish dish is *gópes*, a plateful of tiny bogues.

**Vegetarians** have a more limited choice, although there are excellent dishes such as *fasouláda* (green beans stewed with tomatoes) and *bouréki* (courgette, potato and cheese pie). Local produce surfaces in salads such as the

---

**WATER WARNING**

Bottled water is almost a necessity given the heat of the Cretan summer, but a recent test by the Commerce Ministry found nine Greek brands of mineral water (including the Cretan-produced Zaros brand) contained dangerous substances and were probably simply filled from the factory tap. New regulations to curb these abuses are planned, but meanwhile stick to well-known international brands.

*A fruit and vegetable stall in Iráklion's busy market. Locally grown fruit is delicious and very cheap when in season.*

well-known Greek salad (*horiátiki saláta*, consisting of tomatoes, cucumber, onions and olives topped with crumbly *féta* cheese).

Greeks don't normally order **desserts** with their meal: instead, they head for the local patisserie (*zácharoplasteíon*) for tempting treats such as *baklavá* (pastry filled with nuts and honey), *bougátsa* (pastry filled with a yoghurt/cheese mixture), or *lukumádes* (deep-fried dough balls served with honey).

**Fruit** is plentiful, although much of it is exported. You can feast on cherries, plums, apricots, watermelon, figs, pears, apples, oranges, grapes and even bananas grown locally.

As elsewhere in the Mediterranean, Cretans are not big on **breakfast**, although Continental, English and most other combinations are available in resort areas.

There are plenty of opportunities for snacks such as *souvláki* (often served in pitta bread with salad and yoghurt on take-away stalls), delicious savoury pies filled with cheese or spinach, or Western-style fast food.

## Drinking

The most popular drinking venue for Cretan men is the *kafeníon*, a basic café with a simple interior and tables and chairs outside. The older men of the village happily pass the day here, reading newspapers, arguing politics and playing *távli* (backgammon). It's unusual to see

---

**HANGOVER WARNING**

*Raki* is a clear spirit distilled from the remains of grape pressings in the autumn, with a taste which (according to connoisseurs) varies considerably from village to village depending on the quality of the grapes and the way it's made. Also known as *tsipouro* or *tsikoudhia*, *raki* is never mass-produced. This throat-searing spirit should be treated with caution!

women in the *kafenío*, apart from tourists. In most towns, cities and resorts European-style cafés now serve everything from coffee to cocktails.

The preferred **aperitif** is usually *óuzo* (a clear, aniseed-flavoured spirit which turns cloudy when mixed with water) or *rakí*. Aperitifs are traditionally served with appetizers such as *mezédes*, although as a tourist you'll probably be charged for these. Lager-type **beers** such as Amstel, Löwenbrau and Henniger are brewed locally and are widely available.

The **wine** which most of us remember from our holidays is *retsína*, which has a pungent flavour produced by throwing Aleppo pine resin into the vat of grape juice as it ferments. These resinated wines are incredibly cheap – and at their worst can taste like turpentine – but at their best they have a clean, bright flavour which perfectly reflects the mélange of pine and vine.

Greek table wines are more expensive and, until recently, almost universally bland, but you can now get some interesting bottles from the smaller mainland producers and the bigger companies have been forced to improve quality to keep up: names to watch out for include Domaine Carras, Boutari and Achia Clauss. The best Cretan wine is sold under the Minos Palace label and is produced in Peza-Pediados, a short distance from where the first Minoan vinification plant was discovered.

> ### SWEET COFFEE
>
> Greek coffee (*kafé ellinikó*) is similar to Turkish coffee and is served strong and black in tiny cups, usually with sugar. More sugar is *vari glikó*, without sugar is *skéto*. Instant coffee (usually referred to as 'Nescafé') is available just about everywhere.

*Homemade **rakí** on sale in Iráklion market. The offer of a glass of this clear spirit is a gesture of friendship and you should always accept – and down it – but beware of over-indulgence as it is potent stuff!*

# 2
# Iráklion

Crete's capital city may come as a shock to the senses if you are expecting a tranquil Mediterranean port: it's a huge, noisy, charmless, dusty, concrete conglomeration which bears little resemblance to the rest of the island. The fifth largest city (and the wealthiest per head of population) in Greece, Iráklion is the commercial and business heart of Crete. Cruise liners, container ships and twice-daily ferries from Piraeus dock in the busy port, whilst charter planes stream into the island's main airport, 4km (2.5 miles) from the city centre.

It may sound like a place to avoid but Iráklion still has a sense of energy and vitality about it and a cosmopolitan atmosphere, as well as plenty of shops and a handful of worthwhile sights. The trick to surviving Iráklion is to make sure you're staying somewhere else – dip into what it has on offer, then retreat to the relative peace of the nearby resorts.

The city has had a turbulent past, reflected in its many changes of name since it was founded: the Romans christened the port Heraclium, but with the Arab conquest in AD 824 it became Rabdh el Khandak; it was a pirate's port and one of the biggest slave markets in the Mediterranean.

When the Venetians took over they re-named the city (and the whole island) Candia, and built it up into one of the leading seaports in the eastern Mediterranean, a rich prize for the invading Turks who finally conquered it in 1669. It was only when Turkish rule came to an end in 1898 that the city's original name was re-adopted.

## DON'T MISS

\*\*\* The **Archaeological Museum** (can be combined with a visit to Knossós on most excursions from tourist resorts).
\*\*\* The **icon** collection in the **Ayía Ekateríni**.
\*\* The only painting by **El Greco** in Crete (in the Historical Museum).
\*\* Views of the harbour and city from the top of **Kástro Koúles**, the Venetian Fortress.
\* The daily market in Odhós 1866.
\* Coffee and *bougátsa* in **Platía Venizélou**, overlooking the Morosini Fountain.

**Opposite**: *The Venetian fort at the end of the harbour wall in Iráklion.*

## HISTORY BY NUMBERS

Such is the importance to Cretans of their long struggle for independence over the centuries that they like to name streets after crucial dates on their road to freedom. Thus, in Iráklion you'll find:

• **Odhós 1821**: marks the beginning of the War of Greek Independence.

• **Odhós 1866**: commemorates the year that several hundred martyrs blew themselves up in the Arkádhi Monastery (see page 89).

• **Odhós Avgoústou 25**: the anniversary of the 1898 massacre in Iráklion which led to the expulsion of the Turkish forces from Crete. Over 300 people were killed, including 17 British soldiers and the vice-consul.

## EXPLORING THE CITY

A logical starting-point for exploring Iráklion is on the seafront, where the **old harbour** still shelters a few dozen fishing boats whose catches can be bought straight from the stalls at the top of the sea wall. Directly in front of you, the sea wall leads round to the imposing **Venetian Fort** (see page 40), whilst at the back of the harbour are the old Venetian vaulted **Arsenals** which once served as boat repair sheds.

Leading up into the city from the harbour, the central street of **Odhós 25 Avgoústou** is lined with travel and tour operators, car rental outlets, banks and exchange bureaux and souvenir shops. Near the top, on your left, there's a delightfully spacious plaza which is dominated

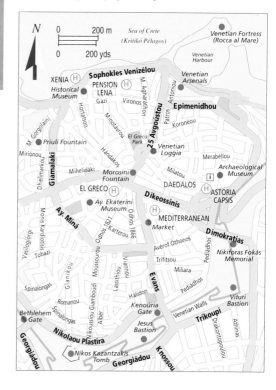

*Dominating a leafy square in the heart of Iráklion, the church of Áyios Títos houses a reliquary containing the skull of St Titus, Crete's first bishop.*

by the church of **Áyios Títos**. The church was originally Byzantine, but has been destroyed and rebuilt many times since it was founded: the Venetians rebuilt it in the 16th century and the Turks later turned it into a mosque. It was destroyed again by an earthquake in 1856 and was finally reconsecrated in 1925.

At the top corner of this square is the stylish **Venetian Loggia**, reconstructed after its destruction in World War II. The original building of 1626 was the focal point of the city for the Venetian aristocracy who held balls and social events here. Walk through the arched passageway of the loggia and you'll find a charming semicircular courtyard behind it – the surrounding rooms now house the offices of the Town Hall.

Almost next door to it is the restored church of **Áyios Markos**, which was built in 1239 but has since been destroyed twice by earthquakes. Rebuilt in 1600, it was later used by the Turks as a mosque; although now a church again, it's also used as an exhibition centre and is well worth a look inside to see what's on.

Áyios Markos overlooks the central square of **Platía Venizélou**. This square is one of the main social hubs of the city, with numerous restaurants and cafés fanning out from the ornate **Morosini Fountain** at its centre. Built in 1628 by Francesco Morosini during the last years of Venetian rule, the fountain incorporates four fine-looking lions from the 14th century.

The fountain rarely seems to flow any more, but

---

**TITUS' ROVING SKULL**

Companion to St Paul when he landed on Crete in AD 59, Titus became the first bishop of Górtyn (see page 59) but was forced to move north when the Saracens landed on the south coast. He was buried in the Church of Áyios Títos in Iráklion on his death, but when the Turks overran Crete in 1669 the Venetians took his skull back home with them for safekeeping. It was only returned from Venice in 1966, and is now one of the church's most prized relics.

*From the tomb of Kazantzakís, a view of Mount Yioúhtas rising up behind the capital. Legend has it that Zeus was buried beneath this mountain, and that the recumbent profile is his.*

political discussions ebb and flow at the surrounding tables over coffee and *bougátsa* – a delicious custard-filled pastry which is the speciality of cafés here.

Directly opposite the Morosini Fountain in the Platía Venizélou, the pedestrianized **Odhós Dedálou** runs up towards the Platía Eleftherías. Dedálou has become one of the trendiest streets in the city, with chic boutiques rubbing shoulders with restaurants and bookstores. **Platía Eleftherías** ('Freedom Square') is another of the city's main hubs, with a leafy garden in the middle, fine views over the city ramparts, and a larger than life-sized bronze statue of Eleftheríos Venizélos, one of the founders of modern Crete.

In one corner of the square is the main **Tourist Information Office** (NTOG), with the huge Archaeological Museum (see page 38) opposite. Tucked away behind the main museum is the new **Battle of Crete and Resistance Museum** (corner of Doukos Bofor and Hatzidaki Streets) which houses an extensive collection of weapons, uniforms, photographs and other items relating to this dramatic period in the island's history.

Continuing southwards from Platía Venizélou brings you to the street known as Odhós 1821, with, parallel to it, Iráklion's **market** in Odhós 1866. Piled high with produce of every description, the busy market is a good place to buy local honeys, yoghurts, home-made *rakí*, packets of herbs, or cheeses and fresh fruit for a picnic.

Jewellery and souvenir shops have taken over from some of the more traditional stalls but it's still a working market for locals who come in from the surrounding countryside for a pair of boots, knives or other essentials.

Further up, side streets lead off to fish and meat stalls: at the top end the market opens out into

*Platía Kournárou, just beyond Iráklion market, is one of several shady squares inviting you to take a break from sightseeing.*

**Platía Kornárou**, with café tables spread out around another lovely fountain – the headless Roman statue built into the fountain comes from Ierápetra. The café itself is housed inside a converted Turkish polygonal kiosk, itself once a fountain. As you sit observing the comings and goings in the market you'll also notice a huge modern sculpture on the far side of the square: the massive figures are those of Erotokritos and Arethousa, a heroic couple from an epic 17th-century poem by Vincenzos Kornáros, after whom the square is named.

Continuing up Odhós Evans you eventually arrive at the **Pórta Kenoúria**, one of the massive, elaborate gates which were completed in the 16th century to defend Crete from the Turks. One glance at the 40m (130ft) thick walls here will give you a good idea of why Iráklion was considered impregnable during this period.

Skirt around inside the wall towards the west and after five minutes' walk you'll see a sign leading up onto the ramparts to the **Tomb of Kazantzakís**. Perched above the city rooftops, the grave of Crete's most famous writer is adorned with a plain cross and a headstone bearing an epitaph from his own writings: 'I hope for nothing, I fear nothing, I am free.' His solitary grave lies here, in unconsecrated ground, because Kazantzakís was scorned by the church for his unorthodox views – although burial rites were performed in the cathedral of Áyios Mínas. There's a great view from here of the easily recognizable profile of **Mount Yioúhtas**.

**MAKING THE MOST OF THE MUSEUM**

The Archaeological Museum can seem overwhelming, and unless you're a serious culture vulture it's best to concentrate on the highlights mentioned here or you risk getting bogged down in an endless succession of pottery displays. Timing is also important: the museum gets horribly crowded and should be avoided by claustrophobics from 11:00 onwards. So come early if possible – or wait until the crush has thinned by around 16:00.

### Archaeological Museum (Archaologikó Mousío) ***

Designed to be earthquake-proof, Iráklion's Archaeological Museum (open winter: Tues to Sun 08:00–17:00, Mon 12:30–17:00; summer: Tues to Sun 08:00–19:00/20:00, Mon 12:00–19:00/20:00, tel: (081) 226-092) looks more like a bunkhouse than the richest repository of Minoan art and artefacts in the entire world – which it can well claim to be, since few items have ever been exported. The museum is old-fashioned, the exhibits poorly labelled, and the presentation and displays very dated (despite recent renovations). Nonetheless, it's a 'must' for any visitor to Iráklion. Finding your way around is largely a question of following the sequence of rooms, which are set out in chronological order.

**Room I** covers the Neolithic Period right up to the advent of the early Minoan or Prepalatial Period (3500–1900 BC; see page 12 for an explanation of Minoan dating). Note the miniature **clay bull** with acrobats vaulting over its horns – early evidence of the Minoan bull cult.

**Room II** spans the First Palace Period (1900–1700 BC), with finds from Knossós, Mália and the peak sanctuaries. Here are the first examples of so-called **Kamáres** pottery, one of the finest styles in prehistoric Greece, with its swirling and elaborate white and red patterns on black backgrounds. **Room III** covers the same period, with the highlight being the celebrated **Phaistós Disk**.

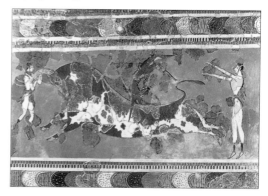

*The Iráklion Museum houses reconstructions of the superb frescoes taken from the Palace of Knossós. This famous image of a charging bull, an animal central to Minoan culture, shows athletes grasping its horns and somersaulting over its back.*

**Room IV** is devoted to the New Palace Period (1700–1450 BC), which was one of the highpoints of Cretan civilization, and several masterpieces from this era are on display here. Amongst them are the **Bull's Head**, a fine example of a ceremonial drinking vessel (known as a *rhyton*). Also here are the famous, bare-breasted **Snake Goddesses** and a delicate ivory model of a **bull-leaper**.

**Room V** is devoted to the final phases of the Knossós palace culture (1450–1400 BC), and includes clay tablets with early **Linear A** and **Linear B** scripts. **Room VI** encompasses finds from graves in the same period, with some magnificent **gold jewellery**. Jewellery is again the main point of interest in **Room VII**, alongside some splendid vases – particularly the gleaming, black **Harvesters' Vase**.

Not to be missed in **Room VIII** is the fabulous **drinking rhyton**, a delicate rock crystal vase with a handle made from pearls. **Room IX** covers finds from eastern Crete (including a large collection of **sealstones**).

Mycenaean influences become more evident in **Room X**, reflecting the decline of the Minoan civilization. The theme is continued in **Room XI**, as the Mycenaeans were defeated by the Dorians, thanks to the first **iron weapons**. Other influences (notably Egyptian) come into play in **Room XII**. **Room XIII** is devoted entirely to **sarcophagi**.

Moving upstairs, **Room XIV** is one of the museum's highlights, with reconstructions of the magnificent **frescoes** which decorated the Palace of Knossós. Also in this room is a wonderful wooden model of the palace, and the striking **stone sarcophagus** from Ayía Triádha – probably one of the most valuable pieces in the museum. **Rooms XV** and **XVI** contain more frescoes, whilst **Room XVII** has exhibits from many different periods.

Back downstairs again, the last three galleries follow through into the Classical, Hellenistic and Graeco-Roman periods.

*The Phaistós Disk, imprinted with hieroglyphics which remain a mystery to archaeologists.*

### THE PHAISTOS DISK

The celebrated Phaistós Disk is one of the many continuing enigmas surrounding Minoan civilization. The 16cm (6in) diameter clay disk is stamped with a series of hieroglyphics on both sides which spiral outwards from the centre. Flowers, birds and human figures can be recognized, but no one knows what they mean; some of the symbols are repeated several times, suggesting that the disk may contain some form of prayer or refrain. Dating from between 1700 and 1600 BC, the symbols were stamped on the disk whilst it was still wet, making it the earliest known example of preclassical printing.

*The church of Ayía Ekateríni houses the most important collection of icons in Crete.*

### Venetian Fortress (Kástro Koúles) ★★★

Guarding the old harbour entrance, this impressive fortress was built by the Venetians between 1523 and 1549 and formed one of their principal defences against the Turkish invaders in the 17th century. It's considered to be one of the most beautiful Venetian fortresses in the Mediterranean.

On entering the fort (open Tuesday–Sunday 09:00–15:00) you swiftly appreciate how the Venetians managed to hold out during 21 years of Turkish sieges, hidden away behind massively thick walls in a series of 26 rooms and turrets which give an air of sheer impregnability. A broad ramp leads up from the interior onto the battlements, from where there are fine views across the harbour and city. On the exterior walls of the carefully refurbished fort are three relief carvings of the Lions of St Mark, emblems of the former Venetian city-state.

### Historical Museum (Istoríke Mousío) ★★

Housed in a neo-classical mansion just back from the seafront to the west of the harbour, the Historical

Museum (open 09:00–15:00 Monday to Friday, Saturday until 14:00, closed Sunday, tel: (081) 283-219) contains an interesting variety of exhibits spanning the centuries from post-Minoan times onwards. On the ground floor there are various 17th-century maps and engravings, with side rooms devoted to weaponry, documents relating to Crete's struggle for independence and rare religious reliquaries and icons. At the back of the main hallway is a small frescoed Byzantine chapel and, next to it, a small room housing just one painting – the only one on Crete by the island's most famous painter, Doménico Theotokópoulos ('El Greco' – see page 51). His *View of Mount Sinai and the Monastery of Saint Catherine* is thought to have been painted around 1570.

The basement houses an assortment of sculpture and stonework from the Byzantine, Venetian and Turkish periods, whilst on the first floor there are displays relating to the German occupation of Crete and replicas of the studies of two other famous Cretans – Níkos Kazantzakís and the politician Emmanuel Tsoúderos, who was Greek Prime Minister during World War II. The top floor houses an excellent collection of textiles, showing a wide variety of styles in weaving, crochet and needlework.

### Platía Ekateríni **

To the west of the market area, this spacious, pedestrianized square is bordered by three churches. The most dominant is the massive **Cathedral of Áyios Mínas**, the largest church in Crete. Built in typical Byzantine-Greek style, it's topped off by two large clock towers and a huge dome. Just below the cathedral is the original **Church of Áyios Mínas**, which contains an elaborate gold altarpiece.

Across the square, the **Ayía Ekateríni** is the most interesting of this trio. Dating from the 15th century, the church (open 09:30–15:00 Monday to Saturday, 17:00–19:00 Tuesday, Thursday and Friday) was an important centre for the arts in the 16th and 17th centuries. The most famous of the paintings now housed inside the church are six icons by Miháilis Dhamaskinós.

---

**ICON STYLES**

At the core of the collection in the Ayía Ekateríni are six paintings by **Miháilis Dhamaskinós**, one of the greatest icon painters of the 16th century. Dhamaskinós was influenced by the so-called 'Cretan Renaissance' which flourished at the monastic school of Ayía Ekateríni until the end of Venetian rule, and is thought to have been a contemporary of El Greco here. Although he lived in Venice between 1577 and 1582 and many of his works show Italian influence in his use of perspective and depth, Dhamaskinós' most admired paintings are those from a later period in a much purer, strictly Byzantine style.

# Iráklion at a Glance

## GETTING THERE

Olympic Airways has six daily flights (flight time 50 minutes) to and from **Athens** (West Terminal). There are also four flights per week to **Rhodes** and three per week to **Thessaloniki**. Regular charter flights operate throughout the summer months from the UK and other European countries. The **airport** is 4km (2.5 miles) east of the city centre. During the peak summer months, with charters arriving and departing at close intervals, the facilities are barely adequate to cope with the number of passengers, but with recent renovations completed in 1995 the situation may improve. In the Arrivals Hall there are *bureaux de change*, a Tourist Information office, and car rental booths. Taxi fares to destinations all over the island are posted in the Arrivals Hall. Bus #1 leaves from the stop opposite the terminal, with frequent departures to central Iráklion (Platía Eleftherías).

**Ferries** from Piraeus dock at the wharves to the east of the old harbour; taxis are available from here to the city centre, otherwise it's a 20-minute walk.

**Buses** from elsewhere in Crete arrive at one of four different bus stations: those from the east arrive at the station opposite the ferry wharf on Odhós Sophokles Venizélou; those from the west arrive at Odhós Grevenon, next to the Historical Museum; services from the southwest arrive the other side of the Haniá gate, on Odhós Pyranthon; services from the southeast arrive at Platía Kíprou, outside the walls at the end of Odhós Evans.

## GETTING AROUND

Most of the major attractions, shops and restaurants in central Iráklion are within walking distance of each other. **Taxis** around the city are reasonably priced, but make sure the meter is running or you agree a price before your journey begins. The main taxi ranks are in Platía Eleftharías and Platía Venizélou; you can also flag down taxis on the streets.

## WHERE TO STAY

*Luxury*
**Grecotel Agapi Beach**, Amoudari, tel (081) 250-502/31108, fax (081) 258-731. On its own private beach 15 mins west of Iráklion (out of town centre); tennis, swimming-pool. (A)
**Astoria Capsis Hotel**, Platía Eleftharías, tel (081) 229-002, fax (081) 229-078. One of the better hotels in Iráklion, centrally located, but try and get a room on the upper floors to avoid traffic noise. (A)
**Galaxy**, 67 Demokratias Ave, tel (081) 238-812, fax (081) 211-211. Well-equipped and very comfortable, with rooms arranged around a courtyard and swimming-pool. (A)

**Xenia**, 5 Odhós Sophokles Venizélou, tel (081) 284-000. Another reasonable choice, in an excellent position on the seafront. (A)
*Mid-range*
**Atrion**, 9 K. Paleológou St, tel (081) 229-225, fax (081) 223-292). Modern and functional, comfortable rooms. (B)
**Mediterranean**, Smirnis St, tel (081) 289-331–4, fax (081) 289-335. Unattractive decor but reasonably priced, fairly quiet and central. (B)
*Budget*
**Olympic**, Platía Kournárou, tel (081) 288-861, fax (081) 222-512. Good value for money in the town centre. (C)
**El Greco**, Odhós 1821, tel (081) 281-071. Long-established hotel, the small rooms are made up for by the fact that most have balconies. (C)
**Daedalos**, 15 Dedálou St, tel (081) 244-812, fax (081) 224-391. Right on Dedálou St (handy for shopping), can be a bit noisy but very good value. (C)
**Metropol**, Karterou 48, tel (081) 242-330. Good value, quiet location near the cathedral. (C)
**Pension Lena**, 10 Lahana St, tel (081) 242-826, fax 242-826. Hidden away down a sidestreet but just a few minutes from Platía Venizélou. Clean and comfortable, good budget choice.

## WHERE TO EAT

**Ciao**, Platía Venizélou, tel (081) 243-958. Large, bright self-service cafeteria on two levels opposite the Morosini Fountain. Breakfasts, snacks and pasta dishes cooked to order. Good value.

**Minos**, 10 Dedálou St, tel (081) 244-827. Popular with locals as well as tourists, good Greek food including specialities such as lamb baked in yoghurt.

**Ippokambos**, Sophokles Venizélou. This busy restaurant at the bottom of 25 Avgoústou has a high reputation for good-value fish dishes and seafood mezédes. It can get very crowded.

**Giovanni**, Korai St, tel (081) 246-338. Atmospheric restaurant hidden away down a quiet alley with some tables outside. Wide range of traditional Cretan dishes as well as a special vegetarian menu.

**Loukoulos**, Korai St, tel (081) 224-435. Italian restaurant with attractive little courtyard (shady by day, candlelit by night). Excellent pizzas and fresh pasta.

**Four Lions**, Platía Venizélou, tel (081) 222-333. Large rooftop café and restaurant above the Morosini Fountain, open all day from breakfast through to cocktails and dinner. Set menus at reasonable prices.

**Ta Leontaria** and **Bougátsa Kirkor**: These two old-fashioned cafés next door to each other on Platía Venizélou are both renowned for their *bougátsa*, a delicious creamy pastry which is served with coffee as a mid-morning

snack – although you can order it any time.

**Dhía Island:** A sailing cruise to this small offshore island is one of the most relaxing excursions in the immediate vicinity of Iráklion. Daily trips on board the *M/S Calypso* include a beach barbeque and stops for swimming. Book through Iráklion travel agents.

**Santorini:** Possibly the most spectacular and photogenic island in Greece, Santorini was formed by a massive volcanic eruption in 1500 BC which sent over half the island plunging to the seabed: the remaining half forms a dramatic semicircle around a series of jagged 'burnt islands', with the beautiful village of Théra perched above the steep cliffs. A funicular railway or donkeys carry visitors up to Théra, and there are other options for excursions on Santorini. The island is about three hours by boat from Crete, with departures at around 07:00 daily (Mon, Tues, Wed, Fri) on board *MTS Artemis*, *P/V John P.* or *MTS Apollo*. Bookings through Iráklion travel agents.

**Island Excursions:** There are

essentially half-a-dozen day trip excursions on Crete which are available from almost any resort or city area. These are: **Knossós**, the **Samariá Gorge**, **Spinalónga Island**, **Phaistós and Górtyn**, the **Lasíthi Plateau**, and **Sitía and Vái Beach**. Since there are so many tour operators offering trips, prices remain reasonably competitive. Well-established tour operators in Iráklion include:

**Adamis Tours**, 23 Odhós 25 Avgoústou, tel (081) 246-202. **Creta Travel Bureau**, 20-22 Epimenidou St, tel (081) 227-002, fax (081) 240-108. **Cretan Holidays**, 36 Dedálou St, tel (081) 242-106, fax (081) 280-608. **Marketos Tours**, 23 Kournárou St, tel (081) 226-727, fax (081) 240-106.

**Tourist Office:** The main EOT office is opposite the Archaeological Museum at 1 Xanthoulidou St, tel (081) 228-225/203, fax 226-020. Open 08:00–14:00 Mon–Fri. **Tourist Police:** tel (081) 246-539/243-466. **Olympic Airways**, Platía Eleftharías, tel (081) 229-191, fax (081) 244-880.

| IRÁKLION | J | F | M | A | M | J | J | A | S | O | N | D |
|---|---|---|---|---|---|---|---|---|---|---|---|---|
| AVERAGE TEMP. °F | 54 | 54 | 57 | 63 | 68 | 75 | 79 | 79 | 73 | 68 | 63 | 57 |
| AVERAGE TEMP. °C | 12 | 12 | 14 | 17 | 20 | 24 | 26 | 26 | 23 | 20 | 17 | 14 |
| Hours of Sun Daily | 5 | 5 | 6 | 7 | 10 | 12 | 10 | 10 | 9 | 7 | 5 | 5 |
| RAINFALL " | 4 | 3 | 2 | 1 | 0.5 | 0 | 0 | 0 | 1 | 3 | 2 | 3 |
| RAINFALL mm | 92 | 69 | 54 | 30 | 15 | 3 | 1 | 1 | 19 | 65 | 57 | 81 |
| Days of Rainfall | 16 | 14 | 12 | 8 | 5 | 1 | 0 | 0 | 2 | 8 | 11 | 15 |

# 3
# Central Crete

Bordered by the Psilorítis Range to the west and the Lasíthi Mountains to the east, central Crete extends from Iráklion on the north coast down to the fertile Plain of Messará and the deserted reaches of the south coast beyond. It's the most heavily visited of the Cretan provinces for the good reason that it holds the greatest concentration of **Minoan sites**, from the wonders of the summer palace at **Knossós** to the winter residences of the Minoan nobility at **Phaistós** and **Ayía Triádha** in the south. Near Phaistós is another important site, the ruins of the Roman town of **Górtyn**.

This region is also home to some of Crete's biggest and brashest beach resorts, such as **Mália** and **Hersónissos**, to the east of Iráklion. To the west there is just the small, upmarket resort of **Ayía Pelayía**, squeezed into a bay beneath the cliffs. In the hinterland here **Tílissos** is another important Minoan site, with the village of **Fódhele**, birthplace of the painter El Greco, comprising another obligatory stop on the tourist circuit.

In the valleys which connect the north and south coasts the Minoans built the first roads. As you travel down these now well-worn routes, glimpses of the old rural Crete reveal themselves: tiny chapels amidst the olive groves and slow-paced mountain villages in which life revolves around the humble *kafenía*.

The south coast has few major resorts or accessible beaches, with the exception of the fast-growing **Mátala**, which has a superb sandy beach beneath a famous series of manmade caves in the sandstone cliffs.

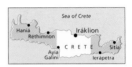

*Sea of Crete*

Haniá · Réthimnon · Iráklion · Sitía · Ayía Galíni · Ierápetra · C R E T E

---

**DON'T MISS**

**\*\*\* Knossós** (usually combined with a visit to the Archaeological Museum in Iráklion).
**\*\*\* Phaistós** and **Górtyn**, on the **Messará Plain** in the south.
**\*\* Lychnostasis Cretan Open-Air Museum**, Hersónissos.
**\* Beaches east of Mália** and west of **Mátala**.

---

**Opposite**: *Characteristic tapering columns at the Minoan palace of Knossós, controversially but evocatively restored by Sir Arthur Evans.*

**IMAGINING THE MINOANS**

Although Evans' controversial reconstructions at Knossós do give an impression of how parts of some buildings may have appeared, it's hard to imagine what this vast, complex palace must have looked like in its entirety. You can get some idea from the cutaway drawings on sale outside the entrance, and also from the scale model on view on the first floor of the Iráklion Museum. However, a far more colourful and detailed picture, both of this site and of others throughout Crete, can be gained from an excellent booklet, *Minoan Crete – An Illustrated Guide with Reconstructions of Ancient Monuments*, by E. Sapouna Sakellaraki (available in local bookshops).

## KNOSSÓS

With about 4200 people crowding in every day at the height of the season, the Minoans' most important palace is not the easiest of places to contemplate in peace. Knossós (open 08:00–17:00 daily, and until 20:00 in the summer months, October–March) lies just 5km (3 miles) outside Iráklion. The best plan, if you want to have it more or less to yourself, is to try to get here first thing in the morning.

Remarkably, the site of this hugely important palace was not revealed until the beginning of the 20th century. Its existence had long been suspected, and the archaeologist Heinrich Schliemann (who discovered ancient Troy) had tried to dig here as early as 1887. Cretan archaeologist Mínos Kalokairinós had unearthed some storage jars on the site and Schliemann speculated that a vast palace existed beneath this small hill. However, he was unable to buy the land and it was left to a young Englishman, Arthur Evans, to claim the glory of Knossós' discovery.

Evans had followed Schliemann's speculations with considerable interest, and after the latter's death in 1890 he set out for Crete to negotiate the purchase of the Knossós land. It took more than five years of tortuous negotiations with the Turkish owners but he finally succeeded, and on 23 March 1900 excavations began. Within a month Evans had discovered the **Throne Room**, and he grandly named the newly discovered civilization

*The Partridge Fresco from the Caravanserai at Knossós. The beautiful glowing colours of the Minoan murals, applied to the walls while the plaster was still wet, were derived from plants, metal oxides and other minerals.*

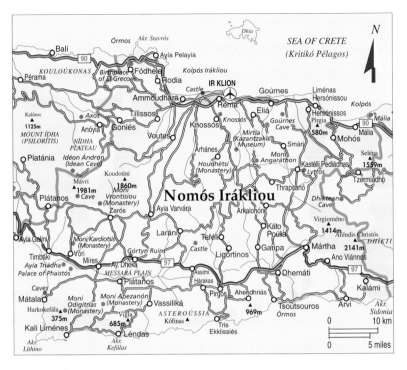

'Minoan' after the great King Minos who had occupied this elegant throne.

One of Evans' most controversial actions during the years he spent digging here was the partial reconstruction of some of the palace buildings. Although this has added to the sense of grandeur of the palace, it has provoked heated debate amongst archaeologists ever since; this kind of work would certainly never be allowed on a site of this importance today, so some might feel it fortunate that the autocratic Evans got away with it then.

Evans was led to 'recreate' parts of Knossós largely because wood had been used extensively in the original palace, not only for beams and rafters but also for the countless pillars, and as he unearthed palace rooms the whole structure was threatened with collapse. Evans at first tried using wood again, as well as brick and stone,

*The bronze bust of Sir Arthur Evans who excavated the palace of Knossós.*

### THE MINOAN LABYRINTH

The legend of the **Minotaur and the Labyrinth** (see page 17) fits well with the structure of the Knossós palace, with its many narrow, dark passageways, stairways that lead up, down and around, and hidden courtyards amongst its 1200 rooms. Whether or not the Minotaur was imprisoned here, when the Greeks first explored the palace after its destruction they found many double-headed axes (*labrys*) engraved on the walls; it's likely that this motif is the origin of the term 'labyrinth', reflecting the puzzling maze of Knossós.

but eventually settled on concrete as being the easiest and cheapest option. He roofed over the **Throne Room**, reconstructed the **Grand Staircase** and the **Central Court** and had French artists repaint the frescoes (which had by then been moved to the Iráklion museum). He also recreated the upper storeys, or **Piano Nobile**, even though there is little evidence to suggest that this was how they might have looked.

### Knossós: Tour of the Site ★★★

Knossós can at first seem overwhelming, even labyrinthine in its complexity, so if your inclination is simply to wander at random you might as well do so – it's not hard to find most of the highlights simply by watching where the guided tours are stopping for explanations.

The first thing that greets you as you enter Knossós is the bust of Sir Arthur Evans, magisterially gazing out over the **West Court**. This may have been a marketplace or even a ceremonial space, since raised walkways lead across it towards the **Corridor of the Procession**. The walls here were once adorned with frescoes of more than 500 figures walking in procession (like most frescoes at Knossós, those you see today are copies). At the end of the corridor a left turn brings you to the **South Propylaea**, once the south entrance to the palace, with frescoes of ritual offerings and characteristic, downward-tapering columns. A wide stairway leads up to what Evans termed the **Piano Nobile**, an upper storey with spacious rooms and a good view over the vast palace storerooms, with their huge clay *pithoi* (storage jars), some of which are still intact.

From this terrace descend to the **Central Court**, the focal point of the palace, where it is thought that bull-leaping contests and other spectator sports may have taken place. In the northwest corner of the court is one of the most fascinating rooms of all, the **Throne Room**. In this surprisingly small room sits the original **Throne of Minos**, with benches for the king's priests running along either side of it and a lustral basin (for ritual purification) opposite; the actual room is now fenced off, but you can still peer inside or pose for photos – as most people do – on the wooden replica which has been placed in the antechamber.

On the other side of the Central Court, the **Grand Staircase** leads up to the **Royal Chambers** in the East Wing. Parts of this wing are closed for repair work, but you can still appreciate how the stairwell brought light

**Opposite:** *The palace larder: these long storage pits contained dozens of the huge clay jars known as* pithoi.

| 1 | Interior Shrine | 12 | Staircase | 23 | Magazine of the Pithoi |
| 2 | Throne Room | 13 | South Propylaeum | 24 | Lapidary's Workshop |
| 3 | Ante Room to the Throne Room | 14 | Corridor of the Procession | 25 | Potter's Workshop |
| 4 | Temple Repositories | 15 | Corridor to the Central Court | 26 | Court of the Stone Spout |
| 5 | Room of the Tall Pithos | 16 | House of the Chancel Screen | 27 | East Bastion |
| 6 | Ante Room of the Pillar Crypts | 17 | Lustral Basin | 28 | Magazines of the Great Pithoi |
| 7 | Square Pillar Crypts | 18 | Queen's Toilet Room | 29 | Corridor of the Draught Board |
| 8 | Corridor of the Magazines | 19 | Queen's Megaron | 30 | Central Court |
| 9 | West Magazines | 20 | Treasury | 31 | North East Magazines |
| 10 | Area of the 'Chariot Tablets' | 21 | Queen's Megaron | | |
| 11 | Temple of Rhea | 22 | King's Megaron | | |

**OLD AND NEW PALACES**

Most of the visible ruins at Knossós belong to the so-called **New Palace**. The first palace was built here around 2000 BC, but was destroyed by an earthquake (along with the palaces at Phaistós and Mália) in about 1700 BC. A hundred years later Knossós had been completely rebuilt, at a time when Minoan civilization was at its peak. It was surrounded by a large town (said to have had a population of 10,000) with two harbours down on the coast. The New Palace and the surrounding town were almost completely wiped out by a mysterious natural catastrophe in 1450 BC.

**OUTLYING RUINS**

There are several other important buildings surrounding the main palace complex; although sadly these are not open to the public. They include the **Caravanserai** (there was a spring here at which travellers could water their animals), the **House of the High Priest**, the **Royal Villa** (to the northeast) and the **Little Palace** (just behind the tavernas on the Iráklion road).

*The village of Ayía Pelayía nestles around a bay of calm clear water ideal for swimming and water-sports.*

into the lower levels, a consistent feature of Minoan design.

At the bottom of the staircase the **Hall of the Colonnades** leads to the **Hall of the Double Axes** and to the so-called **King's Megaron**. Down a short passageway is another of Knossós' most admired features, the **Queen's Megaron**. This is where the famous dolphin fresco was found, leading Evans to presume that this 'feminine' room was that of the queen. Others believe that in fact the royal quarters were in lighter, more spacious apartments on the floors above. A small room leading off to one side housed a 'flushing toilet', with drains leading down to the river.

Further evidence of the ingenious Minoan drainage system can be seen outside to the north of these chambers, where carefully constructed pipes ensure that the waste flow never silted up or flooded. To the north of the royal chambers are the **Palace Workshops**, where potters and jewellers worked, with a **Theatral Area** beyond. Leading from the palace complex the **Royal Road**, paved to allow wagons to move easily, once ran all the way to the port of Amníssos.

### Ayía Pelayía *

Heading west from the capital, the New Road snakes over the hills with fabulous views back over the Bay of Iráklion and the mountains beyond. Past the first headland, a road runs for 3km (2 miles) down to the inviting resort of **Ayía Pelayía**, snug in a sparkling blue bay below.

Ayía Pelayía is dominated by the presence of two smart hotels, the **Peninsula** and the **Capsis**

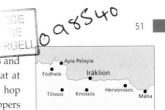

**Beach**. The small, sandy beach is lined with tavernas and bars which are so close to the high water mark that at high tide you might have to take your shoes off to hop from one to the other. It's a popular spot for day-trippers from Iráklion at weekends, with water-skiing, paragliding and other watersports available.

## Fódhele **

Renowned as the birthplace of **El Greco**, Fódhele has been capitalizing on this connection for decades – even though recent research suggests El Greco may have been born in Iráklion. It is, in any case, an attractive village with café tables set out on the river's edge beneath shady plane trees and a wide range of souvenir and craft shops (with lower prices than those in Iráklion). The only testimonial to the painter is a bust and a slate plaque, erected in 1934 by the University of Toledo, in the village square. A short walk outside the village is an old house where he is said to have been born.

## Tílissos *

A large agricultural village in the midst of extensive vineyards, Tílissos is the site of three evocative **Minoan villas** which were amongst the first ancient ruins to be excavated on Crete.

In a wonderful location beneath spreading pine trees, three minutes' walk from the village centre, the villas (open 08:00–14:30 daily, ) were once part of a larger town which flourished at the height of the New Palace Period. Entering **House A**, you find yourself in a courtyard surrounded by a colonnade, with two large storerooms on the north side: note the holes in the base of the *pithoi* here, for tapping oil. Beyond is another room with a lustral basin, and a crypt where three enormous bronze cauldrons were discovered.

Little remains of **House B**, but **House C** still has standing walls and you can explore the various rooms (such as the cult room, storeroom and residential quarters) before taking a look at the cistern and stone altar outside to the north.

### EL GRECO

Born sometime in the early 1540s, the painter Doménico Theotokópoulos, better known as El Greco, left Crete when he was about 25 to study under Titian in Venice. In 1577 he moved to Toledo in Spain, where he built his reputation as one of the greatest exponents of the Spanish Baroque style. He remained in Toledo until his death in 1614, and never returned to Crete.

## Hersónissos *

The first of the major resorts on the north coast, Hersónissos is 27km (17 miles) to the east of Iráklion. It has a long, coarse sandy beach and a wide choice of hotels, restaurants and tavernas (over 100 at the last count) as well as numerous bars and discos – nightlife is what this place is all about, so don't stay here if you're looking for peace and quiet and early nights. There are also plenty of options for beach activities and water-sports, from banana-boat rides to windsurfing and water-skiing. Behind the tavernas on the seafront is a range of trendy boutiques and jewellery shops.

At the eastern end of the resort there are numerous activities, from flume rides to jet-biking and parasailing at the **Star Waterpark** (open 08:00–18:00 daily). One of the newest attractions to open in the area is the **Aquasplash Waterpark** (open 10:00–17:00 daily), about ten minutes' drive up into the hills behind the resort. The entrance fee allows you unlimited use of three giant water slides, 'black hole' flume rides, several pools, children's rides and other water-based activities.

### Lychnostatis Cretan Open-air Museum ***

This interesting new museum deserves to be on every traveller's itinerary when touring or staying in this area. Just 1km (half a mile) outside Hersónissos, **Lychnostatis** (open 08:00–14:30 daily, tel: (0897) 31597) is a 'living museum' where you will gain many informative insights into traditional Cretan culture.

Guided tours (included in the entrance fee) first visit the garden, where you can taste various fruits amongst the aromatic herbs and flowers. You then visit an old Cretan house which has rooms recreated to show typical local lifestyles, with weaving and plant-dyeing workshops below it. Outside again, there's a shepherd's shelter, a threshing-floor and an old windmill. There's also a tiny, whitewashed chapel on the seashore and a café where you can taste wines made on the premises and herbal teas. You can watch Greek dancing and audio-visual shows every Saturday at 21:00.

# Mália *

'From the cradle of civilization – a party!' proclaim the travel brochures, and with some of the hottest nightlife on the island you'll certainly find no shortage of party nights in Mália. The resort is 34km (21 miles) to the east of Iráklion and is even bigger and brasher than Hersónissos, catering to a similar young clientele in search of 'sun 'n' fun'.

One of the longest-established resorts on the island, Mália is spread around a long, sandy beach where most people generally seem to be sleeping off the effects of the night before. There are plenty of watersports available for those able to rouse themselves, but Mália only wakes up at sunset and really begins to get going after midnight: with more than 30 discos and music bars, there's plenty of non-stop action to choose from.

But there is another side to Mália, since it also happens to be the site of one of the four great Minoan palaces. The **Palace of Mália** (open Tuesday to Sunday, 08:30–17:00, closed Monday) lies just to the east of the resort, 3km (2 miles) along the shore. Laid out along roughly the same lines as the other major palaces, it has four wings grouped around a central courtyard.

You enter the site via the **West Court**, with raised pathways which lead southwards across to a set of large circular storage pits (probably used for grain). In the

> ### ESCAPING THE CROWDS
>
> Mália's beaches can get fairly crowded and if you're looking for somewhere more peaceful you should head towards the sand dunes to the east of the resort and just west of the **Palace of Mália**. There's a good sandy beach here which has received a European Blue Flag award for cleanliness, with just one taverna on the other side of the road where you can get refreshments and simple meals. It's about a 40-minute walk from the main resort beaches.

*Once a Roman port and now a thriving resort, Hersónissos is more tranquil during the daytime than by night.*

*The palace of Mália, third largest of the Minoan palaces, was the legendary home of King Sarpedon. It lies in a beautiful and atmospheric setting between the sea and the mountains of Lasíthi.*

other direction the paths lead towards the **North Court**, with a pillared enclosure which it is thought might have been a kitchen; the king's banqueting hall would have been on the floor above. Nearby are the royal apartments, with one of the ritual lustral basins so typical of Minoan palaces. The storeroom holds a pair of enormous, decorated *pithoi*. The **Central Court** is smaller than those at Knossós and Phaistós, with a central pit in the middle which may have been an altar for burnt offerings. On the east side is a **Long Gallery**, with another storeroom behind it.

### Mirtía *

This small agricultural village 12km (7.5 miles) from Iráklion would not be worth the detour but for the fact that it is the birthplace of **Níkos Kazantzakís**, considered to be one of the greatest literary geniuses Crete has ever produced.

In the centre of the village is the unassuming **Kazantzakís Museum** (open 09:00–16:00 daily, closed Sunday and Thursday), whose interior contains an extraordinary testimonial to an extraordinary man. Simply to gaze at the huge quantity of manuscripts, letters, diaries and countless numbers of foreign editions of his works is to realize the depths of his talent and learning: an audiovisual presentation (in either English or Greek) narrates the salient facts of his eventful life. Well worth a visit.

---

**CRETE'S GREATEST WRITER**

Nikos Kazantzakis is best known for his novel *Zorba the Greek* (later turned into a film starring Anthony Quinn), but in fact his output throughout his life was prodigious, encompassing poetry, essays, philosophy, translations of the classics and travel writing. He was born on Crete in 1885, was educated in Athens and then Paris, and spent much of his life travelling. Despite this, his fierce patriotism is evident in much of his work, even though he was excommunicated by the Orthodox Church for his agnostic views. Cretans are intensely proud of the man they consider their greatest writer, and they turned out in their thousands for his funeral procession in Iráklion in 1957.

## Mátala ***

Set on a horseshoe-shaped bay which is perfectly positioned for watching spectacular sunsets, Mátala was first discovered by hippies who lived in the numerous caves carved out of the cliffs on the north side of the beach. Nowadays it's a bustling resort with a predominantly young clientele, and although it gets fairly crowded it's still one of the best choices for a beach resort on the island. Mátala is also very handy for nearby sites such as Phaistós, Ayía Triádha and Górtyn.

The village is rapidly outgrowing its confines on the south side of the bay and hotels are springing up along the approach road down the valley. There are numerous tavernas and restaurants overlooking the beach, and a small **covered market** just off the main street with an excellent selection of crafts and local products.

The **caves** (now only open during daylight hours) are completely manmade, and may have been used as early Christian or Roman tombs. The soft sandstone has been carved to form doorways and windows, and many have beds or benches inside. The hippies who lived here in the 1960s have long since gone, although the occasional bearded type in flowing robes can sometimes be seen meditating at a cave entrance.

If the main beach gets too crowded for comfort, you can scramble over the rocks to **Red Beach**, which has good swimming and is usually almost deserted.

*The soft sandstone cliffs behind the beach at Mátala are honeycombed with ancient manmade caves, inhabited at various times over the centuries, ending with a community of hippies in the 1960s. The caves are now fenced off and accessible only during the day.*

### Phaistós ★★★

The palace of Phaistós (open 08:00–17:00 daily, 08:00–20:00 in summer) enjoys the most spectacular position of all the Minoan palaces. Set on a plateau above the broad Messará Plain, there are sweeping views across these fertile farmlands to the east, with the slopes of Mount Psilorítis (Mount Ídha) rising dramatically to the north.

The second largest palace on Crete after Knossós, Phaistós shares many similarities in its layout and design but, unlike Knossós, there are no fanciful reconstructions here; the excavators have revealed the foundations and the remains of low-lying walls, with little attempt at restoration.

Phaistós was built around 1900 BC and (as with the other palaces) destroyed in 1700 BC; the new palace

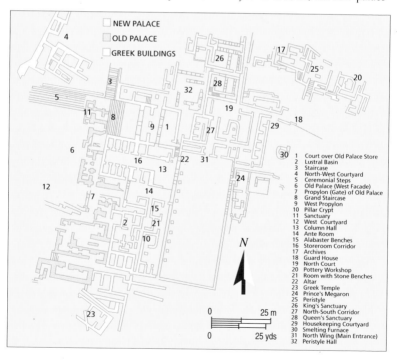

NEW PALACE
OLD PALACE
GREEK BUILDINGS

N

1  Court over Old Palace Store
2  Lustral Basin
3  Staircase
4  North-West Courtyard
5  Ceremonial Steps
6  Old Palace (West Facade)
7  Propylon (Gate) of Old Palace
8  Grand Staircase
9  West Propylon
10 Pillar Crypt
11 Sanctuary
12 West  Courtyard
13 Column Hall
14 Ante Room
15 Alabaster Benches
16 Storeroom Corridor
17 Archives
18 Guard House
19 North Court
20 Pottery Workshop
21 Room with Stone Benches
22 Altar
23 Greek Temple
24 Prince's Megaron
25 Peristyle
26 King's Sanctuary
27 North-South Corridor
28 Queen's Sanctuary
29 Housekeeping Courtyard
30 Smelting Furnace
31 North Wing (Main Entrance)
32 Peristyle Hall

0                25 m

0                25 yds

*The impressive Grand Staircase at the Palace of Phaistós. The 12 steps are 14m (46ft) wide and are partly carved out of the hillside itself.*

which rose from the ruins was occupied until catastrophe again struck in 1450 BC. Parts of both the old and new palaces have been uncovered, making a tour of the site fairly confusing, although the same basic principles apply as they do for the other palaces.

You enter the site just below the tourist pavilion and descend to the **Upper Court**, which leads to the **West Court** and **Theatral Area**. An integral part of the theatral area (it was used for seating) is the magnificent **Grand Staircase**, which was cleverly built with convex steps – raised in the middle and tapering towards each end – to enhance its appearance. At the top of the steps is the west entrance to the **New Palace**, with a series of seemingly cramped rooms overlooking the storerooms of the **Old Palace**.

You come next to the magnificent **Central Court**, with its panorama over the surrounding countryside; in the northwest corner there's an unusual stepped rostrum which it is thought may have been used by athletes to spring off when grabbing the bulls' horns during the bull-leaping spectacles. North of the courtyard are the **royal apartments**, illuminated by the same type of light-wells found at Knossós. Although there are no elaborate frescoes, the king's and queen's rooms were built with fine alabaster panelling and floors which must have had an impressive effect. Nearby is the usual **lustral basin**, for ritual cleansing.

---

### FERTILE FLATLANDS

**Phaistós** was well placed for food supplies, perched as it was above the huge **Messará Plain**, one of Crete's most fertile and productive agricultural areas. Sheltered between the Psiloritis Range to the north, the Dhiktean Mountains to the east and the Kófinas Hills to the south, the Messará Plain is irrigated by two great rivers, the Yeropótamos and the Anapodaris. First occupied during Neolithic times, it became the centre of economic activity on the island when Phaistós was built. Later, the Romans took advantage of the plain's rich soils when they built their island capital at **Górtyn** on its northern edge. Today the plain is used to grow olives, vegetables, fruit (including pineapples, bananas and kiwi fruit) and even coffee. Such is the soil's fertility that even **wild flowers** are said to grow larger and taller here than they do elsewhere on the island.

*The Harvesters' Vase, discovered at Ayía Triádha, depicts a procession of farmworkers and musicians returning from the fields.*

Continuing to the northeast you arrive at the palace workshops and the **Treasury**, where the famous **Phaistós Disk** was found (it is now in the Iráklion Museum).

### Ayía Triádha **

Around the other side of the hill, 3km (2 miles) from Phaistós, Ayía Triádha (open 08:00–19:00/20:00, tel: (0892) 91360) is also in a spectacular setting – this time facing the delta of the Yeropótamos River on the Messará Plain.

Built sometime after the first palace at Phaistós, Ayía Triádha remains something of a puzzle: it doesn't follow the usual pattern of Minoan palaces, and in any case what would be the point of building another palace so close to Phaistós? It may have been the country estate of a prince or nobleman, or it may have had some other ritual significance.

Entering the site you come into the large **Upper Court**, from where you can gain a good impression of the L-shaped palatial buildings on the north and west sides. On a hillock to the south is a small Byzantine chapel, **Ayios Yíoryios**, which has fragments of some fine frescoes.

In the corner of the L-shape are some of the most interesting rooms, including an **inner chamber**, with well-preserved wall panelling, and a **bedroom** with a raised gypsum platform in the middle.

To the north of the palace site are the remains of a **township**, with a series of eight identical **shops** running down the hill: this is the only known example of a Minoan market. Beyond here is the **cemetery**.

### Vóri ***

The main reason for visiting this village is the brilliant **Museum of Cretan Ethnography** (open 10:00–18:00 daily) which houses a superb collection of traditional items, ranging from weavings to basketwork, stretching back hundreds of years. Everything is immaculately displayed, with clear labelling in English. As well as a rich collection of weavings, there are traditional ceramics,

---

**FAMOUS FINDS**

Whatever the purpose of **Ayía Triádha** might have been, its significance is undisputed since it has yielded up some of the most precious **Minoan artworks** found anywhere on Crete. These include the famous carved black steatite vases such as the **Harvesters' Vase** and the **Chieftain Cup** (which can be found in Room VII in the Iráklion Museum) as well as the unusual **fresco** of a cat stalking a pheasant and the celebrated Ayía Triádha painted **sarcophagus** (Room XIV) found in the cemetery.

domestic utensils, old weaponry, musical instruments, old farm tools and many other curiosities. The museum won a commendation in the European Museum of the Year Awards in 1992, and should be included on any itinerary passing near Phaistós.

### Górtyn ***

Just outside the town of **Áyii Dhéka** on the Messará Plain, Górtyn (open 08:00–19:00 daily, tel: (081) 226-092) is, just for a change, not a Minoan site. Initially occupied by the Dorians, it later rose to prominence under the Romans and became the capital of not only Crete itself but also the province of Cyrenaica, encompassing Egypt and other parts of North Africa as well.

The most important part of the site lies within a fenced enclosure to the north of the road, where the first building you see is the large **Basilica of Áyios Títos**. Only the main apse and two side apses survive, but the outline of this impressive church is easy to make out. Further on is the well-preserved and impressive **Odeon**, a semicircular theatre with a marble floor and tiers of marble seats. At the back of the theatre are the famous **Law Codes of Górtyn**, incorporated into a wall built by the Romans.

Górtyn was once a substantial city, and further remains are scattered over the olive groves on the south side of the main road and beyond on the hill.

> **THE LAW CODES**
>
> These engraved stone tablets represent the first written code of law in Europe, dating from around 500 BC. Comprising some 17,000 letters in Doric Cretan dialect, the codes express the conservatism of Dorian society and deal with the relationships between citizens and slaves, adultery, rape, inheritance, trade and property. The codes (which read from left to right and then right to left again) have much to teach about society in ancient Crete.

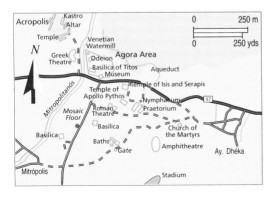

# Central Crete at a Glance

## GETTING THERE

See p 42 for flight and boat connections to Iráklion. Transfer times to the resorts are: **Ayía Pelayía**, 30 min; **Hersónissos**, 45 min; **Mália**, 1 hr; **Mátala**, 1 hr 45 min.

## GETTING AROUND

Frequent buses run along the New Road to Iráklion from the north coast resorts. If you're staying on the north coast you'll have to go to Iráklion to catch buses to destinations in central Crete. **Knossós** is a 20-min bus ride from Platía Venizélou in central Iráklion (bus #2 runs every 10 min). Buses also run to **Fódhele** and **Tílissos** from the Haniá Gate terminal, although not that regularly. **Mirtía** is more easily reached by hire car. There are around 6 buses daily from Iráklion to **Mátala**. Frequent services run from Iráklion to **Míres**, where you change buses for the last 6km (4 miles) to **Górtyn**. **Phaistós** is served by around 9 buses a day from Iráklion, and **Ayía Triádha** is a 40-min walk around the hill from Phaistós. If you are not hiring a car, these three sites are probably most easily visited as part of a day tour (see **Excursions**).

Car rental agencies in **Hersónissos** include **Eurorent**, 177 and 216 Venizélou St, tel (0897) 24370, **Car Plan**, 143 Venizélou St, tel (0897) 24597 and **Zákros Cars**, Venizélou St, tel (0897)

22137. In **Mália**, try **Sunny Holidays**, 9, 25 Martioy, tel (0897) 31913, **Mália Cars** tel (0897) 31285 or **Skyline**, 83 Venizélou St, tel (0897) 31715.

## WHERE TO STAY

### Ayía Pelayía
*Luxury*
**Capsis Beach Hotel**, Ayía Pelayía 71500, tel (081) 811-112, fax (081) 811-076. Superb resort complex with bungalows scattered around a headland, two pools and full facilities, including an open-air theatre on promontory. (A)
**Peninsula Hotel**, PO Box 1215, Iráklion 71110, tel (081) 811-313, fax (081) 811-291. Not quite as grand as the Capsis, but also in a good position with access to its own small beach. Pool, watersports, tennis. (A)
**Alexander House**, PO Box 1392, Ayía Pelayía 71500, tel (081) 811-303, fax (081) 811-381. Almost in the centre of Ayía Pelayía, a modern hotel with extremely comfortable facilities. (A)
*Mid-range*
**Hotel Panorama**, PO Box 1356, Ayía Pelayía 71500, tel (081) 811-002, fax (081) 811273. Set on the hillside above Ayía Pelayía, with (as the name suggests) sweeping views of the bay. Pool. Rooms are straightforward, and it's a fair hike to the beach. (B)

### Hersónissos
*Luxury*
**Creta Maris**, Hersónissos

70014, tel (0897) 22115, fax (0897) 22130. On the (better) western end of the beach, combining vernacular architecture with luxury facilities. Pool, tennis, watersports.
**Knossós Royal Village**, Hersónissos 70014, tel (0897) 23375, fax (0897) 23150. On the beach, with two huge swimming-pools, a waterfall and waterslide. Full sports and watersports facilities. (De luxe)
**Golden Beach**, Hersónissos 70014, tel (0897) 22391. Friendly, well-managed hotel close to the centre of the action. Rooftop pool, beach bar, watersports. (A)
**Silva Maris**, Hersónissos 70014, tel (0897) 22850, fax (0897) 21404. Attractive complex around a large pool; own beach area, watersports, tennis. (A)
*Mid-range*
**Sun Marine**, Hersónissos 70014, tel (0897) 24623. Friendly seafront hotel with reasonably priced rooms. (B)
**Maria Apartments**, Hersónissos 71004, tel (0897) 22580. Family-run, spacious apartments with a small pool, 400m (450yd) from beach. (B)
*Budget*
**Hotel Iro**, Hersónissos 71004, tel/fax (0897) 22136. Right in the centre of Hersónissos, so can be noisy. (C)

### Mália
*Luxury*
**Grecotel Mália Park**, Mália 70007, tel (0897) 31461, fax (0897) 31460. 1.5km (1 mile) outside Mália with bungalows

# Central Crete at a Glance

in a beautiful garden setting on the edge of the beach. The hotel has full facilities and the usual high standards of the Grecotel group. (A)

*Mid-range*

**Hotel Triton**, Mália 70007, tel (0897) 32210. Modern, friendly hotel close to the centre of Mália but reasonably quiet and peaceful. Pool. (B)

**Sun Beach**, Mália 70007, tel (0897) 31401. On one of the best parts of the beach, 1.8km (1 mile) from the centre of Mália. No pool. (B)

*Budget*

**Hotel Mália**, Mália 70007, tel (0897) 31564, fax (0897) 31565. 800m (875yd) from the beach, peaceful yet handy for the resort centre. Rooms are in a large block overlooking the pool. (C)

**Hotel Frixos**, Mália 70007, tel (0897) 31941. 1.5km (1 mile) from the beach, efficiently run hotel with well-furnished rooms; pool. (C)

**Pension Aspasia**, Mália 70007, tel (0897) 22889. Long-established, friendly pension just outside the old village. Clean and reasonably priced. (C)

*Mátala*

*Mid-range*

**Orion**, Mátala 70200, tel (0892) 42129. Stylish little hotel tucked away in the valley behind Mátala; very peaceful. Pool. (B)

*Budget*

**Hotel Zafira**, Mátala 70200, tel (0892) 45112, fax 45725. Close to the action, comfort-

able and affordable. (C)

**Hotel Europa**, Mátala 70200, tel (0892) 42361. Small, friendly hotel surrounded by gardens and yet within easy reach of the beach. (C)

WHERE TO EAT

*Hersónissos*

**La Fontanina**, Georgiou Petraki St, tel (0897) 22209. Very good pizzeria/spaghettaria just off the main street.

**Sokaki**, 10 Evagelistias St, tel (0897) 23972. Reasonably priced taverna with Cretan specialities.

**La Pergola**, 11 Georgiou Petraki St, tel (0897) 23738. Popular taverna down a side-street, Cretan dishes and Greek barbeques a speciality.

**New China Restaurant**, Georgiou Petraki St, tel (0897) 23025. Busy Chinese restaurant with wide menu.

*Mália*

**Old House Tavern**, 25 Arkadioy St, tel (0897) 32128. One of the best restaurants in the old village; nice leafy courtyard, Greek and international dishes.

**Petros**. Another atmospheric restaurant near Platia Ayios Dhimitri in the old village, good for steaks and fish.

**Romantic Raphael**, near

Platia Ayios Dhimitri. Quiet restaurant with a terrace and garden, wide range of dishes including Asian specialities, grills and the usual Greek fare.

**San Georgio**, tel (0897) 32211. On the main square in the old village, with an upstairs terrace draped in bougainvillaea. Family-run, traditional Greek dishes.

### TOURS AND EXCURSIONS

Mália and Hersónissos are well-stocked with travel agents offering excursions to **Samariá**, **Iráklion** and **Knossós**, **Ayios Nikólaos** and **Spinalónga**, as well as the 'southern triangle' of **Phaistós**, **Górtyn** and **Mátala**. Reliable operators include **Kourkounis Tours**, tel (0897) 24665, **Selena Tours**, tel/fax (0897) 33316, and **Zákros Tours**, tel (0897) 22137.

**Aquamarine Tours**, tel (0897) 32259, run various sea cruises (including excursions to **Sissi Island**, **Móhlos** and **Psira Island** and **Dhía Island**).

### USEFUL CONTACTS

**Tourist Office**, 19 Eleftherias St, Hersónissos, tel (0897) 22202.

| SOUTH COAST | J | F | M | A | M | J | J | A | S | O | N | D |
|---|---|---|---|---|---|---|---|---|---|---|---|---|
| AVERAGE TEMP. °F | 55 | 55 | 57 | 63 | 70 | 77 | 82 | 82 | 77 | 70 | 64 | 59 |
| AVERAGE TEMP. °C | 13 | 13 | 14 | 17 | 21 | 25 | 28 | 28 | 25 | 21 | 18 | 15 |
| Hours of Sun Daily | 5 | 5 | 7 | 11 | 11 | 12 | 13 | 12 | 10 | 8 | 6 | 5 |
| RAINFALL " | 4 | 3 | 9 | 1 | 0.5 | 0 | 0 | 0 | 0.5 | 2 | 2 | 4 |
| RAINFALL mm | 109 | 78 | 50 | 23 | 11 | 1 | 0 | 0 | 16 | 44 | 60 | 113 |
| Days of Rainfall | 13 | 11 | 8 | 5 | 3 | 0 | 0 | 0 | 5 | 5 | 7 | 13 |

# 4
# Eastern Crete

The narrow, eastern end of the island juts out beyond the Dhíkti Massif which separates it from central Crete, with the biggest and most popular resort at **Áyios Nikólaos** nestling in the shelter of the beautiful **Bay of Mirabéllo** on the north coast. At the beginning of this century Áyios Nikólaos became the capital of Lasíthi Province but still remained a relative backwater until international tourism arrived in the 1960s. Since then it hasn't looked back, capitalizing unashamedly on its delightful surroundings to become one of the island's top resorts.

Almost all the places of interest in this area – from the haunting ruins of **Spinalónga Island** to the unusual landscapes of the **Lasíthi Plateau** and the fabulous frescoes in the **Panayía Kirá** – can easily be reached from Áyios Nikólaos, but there are plenty of alternatives if you prefer to be based somewhere less crowded.

Following the dramatic coast road east from Áyios Nikólaos brings you to the ancient port of **Sitía**, a good jumping-off point for beaches (such as the palm beach at **Vái**) and traditional villages on the far eastern coast. Eastern Crete also has its fair share of noteworthy Minoan sites, particularly the **Palace of Zákros** at the end of the metalled road on the eastern tip of the island.

The south coast, which is easily reached across the narrow isthmus from **Gourniá** in the Bay of Mirabéllo, is characterized by mile upon mile of greenhouses behind the beaches, with the town of **Ierápetra** (which is one of the hottest places in Crete) the main focus for tourism.

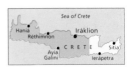

| DON'T MISS |
| --- |
| ★★★ A tour of the **Lasíthi Plateau**. |
| ★★★ A boat trip to **Spinalónga Island**. |
| ★★ Frescoes in the **Panayía Kirá**. |
| ★★ Lunch on the seashore at **Káto Zákros**. |
| ★ Buying a weaving in **Kritsá**. |

**Opposite**: *Embroidered clothes, table linens and weavings for sale garland the doorways of houses in the mountain village of Kritsá.*

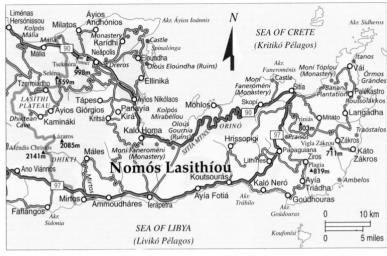

### Áyios Nikólaos ***

One of the longest-established resort towns in Crete, Áyios Nikólaos enjoys a fabulous setting in the **Bay of Mirabéllo** which has entranced visitors for decades. Built around a small, hilly peninsula, one of the main attractions of Áyios Nikólaos is the unusual juxtaposition of its fishing harbour and picturesque **Lake Voulisméni** which lies just behind it. A plethora of restaurants, hotels and shops have sprung up around the lake, harbour and coastline, creating one of the busiest, liveliest resorts on Crete – known affectionately as 'Ag Nik' to regulars.

The focal point of the town is Lake Voulisméni, surrounded by steep cliffs and greenery and connected to the harbour by a canal dug by the Turks in the 1870s. On the far side of the lake is a little path which leads up to the clifftops, where you can sit and contemplate Voulisméni and the rooftops of Áyios Nikólaos.

Behind the main row of cafés and restaurants on the lake-shore are two shady, tree-lined streets (Koundoúrou Roussou and 28 Octóvriou) where you'll find a good selection of ceramic, leatherwork and souvenir shops. Both streets end up at Platía Venizélou, where there is a war memorial commemorating 400 local citizens who

---

**REACHING THE BEACH**

Áyios Nikólaos is renowned for its nightlife rather than its beaches, most of which are outside town and require some effort to reach.
• In the town itself you can swim in the little bay known as **Kitroplatía** over the headland from the harbour.
• On the other side of the bus station there's a small, sandy beach but it does get very crowded.
• Your best bet is to keep going south to the municipal beach at **Almirós**, which is clean and sandy and reached via a 2km (1 mile) footpath or along the road around the bay.

were shot by the Germans in 1943. Beyond is the KTE bus station and the main town beach.

Back on the west side of the port, the seafront road circles a small bay and continues to **Eloúndha** (see page 68); along this coastline are some of the smarter hotels, with low-rise bungalow complexes hidden away on the headlands amongst groves of olives and bougainvillaea.

## Archaeological Museum **

A steep walk up Konstantínou Paleológou from the lake brings you to the Archaeological Museum (open Tuesday–Sunday 08:00–14:30, closed Monday) which houses a wealth of Minoan and other artefacts from the numerous sites in eastern Crete. The museum is spacious and well-lit and rarely seems crowded, so you can have a good look around without being swamped by other visitors.

The rooms are arranged in chronological order: **Room 1** contains a number of early Minoan daggers; **Room 2** has displays of some fascinating figurines, notably the unusual Goddess of Mírtos in the form of a libation jug; **Room 3** holds a number of decorated clay sarcophagi (*larnakes*) as well as an outstanding, intricately decorated stone vase in the form of a Triton shell. In **Room 4** you'll find another unusual exhibit, a clay *pithoi* (vase) which was used for an infant burial: it was transported here (complete with skeleton) in one piece, and is presented precisely as it was discovered by the archaeologists. Clay animals and figurines in **Room 5** complete the Minoan exhibits, whilst **Rooms 6** and **7** contain Greek and Roman finds: the star exhibit is a skull adorned with a wreath of thin, beaten gold with which it was buried.

> **THE BOTTOMLESS LAKE**
>
> The deep, aquamarine waters of **Lake Voulisméni** are said to harbour many secrets – it was once thought to be bottomless (hence its alternative local name, Xepatoméni, 'the bottomless one') but soundings have since revealed that it is in fact 64m (210ft) deep. Legend has it that this is where Britomartis and the goddess Athena once bathed together. Early this century sulphur fumes were discovered rising from the lake bottom, leading some people to believe it was connected by an underground passage to volcanic Santoríni; the Germans are thought to have ditched tanks and weapons in its waters, but no trace has ever been found.

*Picturesque Lake Voulisméni, at the heart of the resort of Áyios Nikólaos.*

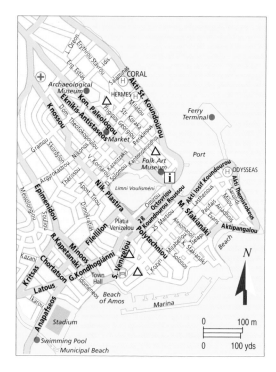

## Folk Art Museum ★★

Conveniently located just next door to the Tourist Information Office, the Folk Art Museum (open 10:30–13:30 and 18:00–21:30 daily, closed Sunday) houses a fine little collection which it is well worth popping in to see.

Old photographs convey the atmosphere of Áyios Nikólaos before the boom, and there are many interesting artefacts garnered from surrounding villages which give a flavour of times gone by. Some of the best exhibits are the magnificent handwoven and embroidered textiles from the region.

## Panayía Kirá ★★★

This lovely whitewashed church set in an olive grove and surrounded by sinuous cypresses contains some of the most complete and well-preserved Byzantine frescoes on Crete (open 08:00–14:30 Tues–Sun, tel: 0841-51525).

The frescoes date back to the 13th and 14th centuries, with the oldest ones found in the central nave of the church. The dome is decorated with scenes from the gospel in traditional, restrained Byzantine style, with the gospel story continuing on the vaulted roof where *The Last Supper* features a particularly unpleasant-looking Judas. In the south aisle the paintings follow the life of Anne, mother of Mary, and Mary's story up until the journey to Bethlehem. The pictures here are far livelier, with the faces full of expression and drama. In the last aisle there is an impressive *Second Coming*.

---

### GET THERE EARLY

The impressive frescoes in the **Panayía Kirá** are well worth looking at in some detail, but try to go early in the morning because the somewhat cramped interior of the church soon fills up with tour groups later on. At the souvenir stall outside you can buy an excellent, illustrated book – *Panayía Kirá: Byzantine Wall Paintings at Kritsá* by M. Borboudakis – which explains them in depth.

## Lató *

Just before you reach Kritsá a signposted road off to the right leads up to the Dorian site of Lató (open 08:00–14:30 Tues–Sun) perched on a rocky saddle high above the plains. After climbing up from the entrance gate you arrive at a courtyard surrounded by massive, crumbling walls and the remains of a theatre, shrines, and the *archontes* or town hall. A broad set of steps leading up between the ruins of two watchtowers leads to a raised terrace from where there are spectacular views over the **Dhiktean Mountains** and Áyios Nikólaos.

## Kritsá *

Sprawling across the mountain slope with panoramic views back down towards the coast, this large village has benefited enormously from the proximity of the **Panayía Kirá** and has become an obligatory stop for day-trippers visiting the church. The long, winding main street in the village is bedecked with weavings and embroideries hung out above people's doorways, and you can pick up some relative bargains here in rugs, table linens and shawls if you haggle hard. Ceramics and leatherwork are also available at prices which are often lower than those found in Áyios Nikólaos. There is a pleasant and shady little square halfway up the main street where you can take a break between bargaining for handicrafts.

| THE REAL THING |
| --- |

Kritsá has long been famous for its **weavings** but many of the designs now cater to mass market tastes, featuring the ubiquitous dolphins and windmills. If you want a really authentic item, look for geometric patterns or those in natural wool colours such as brown, cream or grey, in which the subtleties of the wool provide pleasing effects.

*The central nave of the beautiful Byzantine church of Panayía Kirá dates from the mid-13th century, as do the oldest of the magnificent frescoes it contains.*

## Eloúndha *

At the northern end of the **Bay of Mirabéllo** 8km (5 miles) north of Áyios Nikólaos, Eloúndha has also grown rapidly in recent years into a thriving resort. Although more low-key than Ag Nik, it does have several smart hotels nearby – which may well account for its popularity with Greek politicians.

At the centre of the village is a large fishing harbour, now bordered on three sides by tavernas, shops and hotels; on one side of the harbour there's a sandy/pebbly beach with some watersports available. The bay is well protected, thanks to the **Spinalónga Peninsula** which juts out to the north; it's usually known as 'big Spinalónga' to distinguish it from **Spinalónga Island** (see opposite).

From the outskirts of Eloúndha a narrow causeway leads across to the peninsula, which has several points

of interest and makes for an enjoyable walk. On either side of the causeway are the remains of **Venetian salt pans**, interspersed with several small beaches; crossing a narrow bridge onto the peninsula itself there's an old **windmill** directly ahead, with a small taverna and a popular beach on the right-hand side. Just behind here is the excavated **mosaic floor** of an early Christian basilica, with some well-preserved designs of dolphins, fish and flowers. The church was once part of the ancient city of **Oloús** and if you continue to the right you can see traces of the old harbour, now submerged beneath the sea. There are plenty of secluded spots for sunbathing on the rocks around this side of the peninsula.

### Spinalónga Island ★★★

This rocky island dominates the entrance to Eloúndha Bay, forming a natural bastion of which the Venetians took advantage in 1579 by building an almost impregnable coastal fort on its heights. With its 35 cannons the fortress held out for more than 40 years after the rest of Crete had fallen to the Turks, and was only finally handed over by treaty in 1714. Several Turkish families settled here in the 19th century, but their descendants were forced to move in 1903 when the Cretan government decided to turn the island into a leper colony.

It is this slightly ghoulish connection which forms part of the attraction for the scores of tour boats which now visit Spinalónga every day (mostly from Áyios Nikólaos). Needless to say there is no risk of infection, and indeed visiting Spinalónga is not quite as morbid as it sounds. The ruins of the former leper colony are a poignant reminder of the suffering of its sick inhabitants and the courage with which they bore their illness in the unenlightened days before a cure was discovered for Hansen's Disease (as it is now known).

### Lasíthi Plateau ★★★

Featuring on countless postcards and travel brochure covers, the white-sailed windmills of the Lasíthi Plateau have almost become symbols for Crete itself. Apart from those outside tavernas aiming to attract passing custom,

---

**THE OLD LEPER COLONY**

About 400 Cretan lepers, plus others from elsewhere in Greece, were initially settled on Spinalónga, rebuilding the old Venetian and Turkish houses and creating gardens with goats and chickens. They renovated the old reservoirs of the fort and eventually a small village grew up, with its own church, tavernas and shops. In 1937 a hospital was built, and it wasn't until 1957 that the colony was closed down and the remaining residents taken to an Athens hospital.

**Left:** *The massive fortifications on Spinalónga Island were built by the Venetians in the 16th century as part of their defences against the Turks.*

**Opposite:** *A dramatic play of sun and shadow on the coast near Eloúndha.*

few of these windmills still exist today. However, that doesn't stop dozens of coaches and hire cars grinding their way up the twisting mountain roads for a day out in Lasíthi – and there are other compensations. The plateau itself, for instance, is a spectacular sight: this huge circular plain, flat as a pancake, is surrounded by the towering mass of the **Dhíkti Mountains**, and there are only two routes over the high passes to reach it. Once over the mountains the whole plateau is laid out beneath you like a little kingdom in miniature, with a series of small villages huddled around the patchwork of fields at the centre of Lasíthi. The **Dhiktean Cave** (see opposite) is also a major attraction.

Thanks to fertile soil and natural underground water reservoirs farming has prospered for centuries on this 60km² (21 sq mile) plain and almost anything can be grown here: the main crops are apples, pears, wheat, potatoes and other vegetables. At one time over 10,000 white-sailed windmills pumped water across these fields, but nowadays the farmers mostly rely on diesel pumps and the windmills have fallen into disuse.

Once you reach the plateau it's immediately obvious that the whole area is a natural fortress, and the Cretans have taken advantage of this asset many times – most notably retreating here from the Venetians during the 13th century and the Turks in the 19th century.

## THE BIRTH OF ZEUS

When Rhea hid Zeus in the **Dhiktean Cave** to save him from the terrible fate of being eaten by his father (see page 16) she protected him by getting the Kouretes to beat their drums whenever he cried. Later, when Zeus himself became ruler of the world, he received his son Minos here to instruct him in the art of kingship.

Approaching Lasíthi up the road from Mália you breach the mountain rim over the **Pass of Ambélou** at 1046m (3433ft) where the remains of several stone-built windmills are strung out on either side of the road: these are former grain mills, strategically placed to take advantage of the strong northerly *meltémi* winds.

Descending onto the plain and turning right, you pass through several villages on the road circling the plain until arriving at **Psychró**, where a sign leads up to the **Dhiktean Cave** (open 08:00–19:00/20:00 daily).

Supposedly the birthplace of **Zeus**, this is the most famous cave on the island and well worth visiting. The track up through an oak forest to the entrance of the cave is not too difficult (it takes about 20 minutes; you can hire a donkey if you want to be carried up) but the steps down into the black depths of the cave can be very tricky – especially after rain. A guide isn't obligatory, although if you haven't brought your own torch you'll find it helpful to have someone with a lamp.

The 70m (230ft) deep canyon is certainly impressive, and it's easy to conjure up the myths and legends which have become associated with it amongst the stalactites and stalagmites.

Continuing from Psychró you come to **Áyios Giórgios**, a small village with an atmospheric little **Folk Museum** (open 10:00–16:00 daily, summer only). Housed inside a 19th-century village dwelling, the museum provides an interesting insight into the Cretan way of life in the last century.

Finally, the road leads you to **Tzermiádho**, Lasíthi's main village, where there are plenty of handicraft shops as well as tavernas and cafés.

## Moní Faneroméni *

Heading eastwards from Áyios Nikólaos the road winds its way gradually up above the jagged cliffs, skirting the occasional beach way down below, with views all the way back across the Bay of Mirabéllo as far as Spinalónga Island. There are a couple of interesting places to stop along the way, and this would make a

**Opposite:** *Lasíthi is famous for its windmills, thousands of which were once used to draw water from underground reservoirs beneath the plateau.*

---

**WATER TABLES**

The Lasíthi Plateau is fed by melting snow from the surrounding mountains during the spring, when the whole plateau is often flooded and only trees and windmills project above the surface of the water. The floods drain away through clefts in the rock into vast reservoirs in the limestone beneath, and during the summer the windmills were formerly used to pump it back up again for irrigation. In the last twenty years most windmills have been replaced by more reliable pumps, partly to compensate for a falling water table. A large above-ground reservoir has also been built to the south of the plateau to supplement the underground supply.

**THE LOST CITY**

The original name of the Minoan town at Gourniá has long been lost in the sands of time, but it's thought that it was occupied from the early Bronze Age onwards. Arthur Evans suspected that there was something substantial buried here but it was left to Harriet Boyd Hawes, a young American archaeologist, to carry out the excavation between 1901–4.

*Perched precariously high above the plains, Moní Faneroméni houses some interesting frescoes and offers spectacular views over the sea.*

pleasant excursion culminating in a seafood lunch at the tiny port of **Móhlos**.

Signposted to the right off the main road, 16km (10 miles) from Áyios Nikólaos, the Moní Faneroméni is at the end of a 6km (4 mile) dirt track which needs to be tackled with care. However, the drive is worth it if only for the spectacular views from this isolated monastery perched like an eagle's eyrie on a rocky ledge high up above the plains of **Kaló Chorió**, with the **Gulf of Mirabéllo** beyond.

The monastery was built around a small hermit's grotto where a sacred icon of the Virgin was discovered in the 15th century, and the chapel which encloses the grotto in the cliff-face also houses some impressive frescoes from this period. The caretaker will unlock the chapel for a small consideration, but occasional electricity failures mean that you may have a hard time deciphering the frescoes by candlelight – bring your own torch to be on the safe side!

## Gourniá **

After descending from the monastery, the archaeological site of Gourniá (open 08:00–14:30 Tuesday–Sunday, tel: 0841-24943) is clearly signed a little further along the road.

This is one of the most evocative archaeological sites on Crete, partly because the narrow, cobbled streets and the remains of houses leading off them are so well preserved: unlike the grand palace sites, which require considerable imagination to envisage them in their heyday, this everyday Minoan town bears many similarities to present-day mountain villages on the island.

It's thought that the ancient town once stretched all the way down to the sea, and by the number of fish-hooks,

*The beautiful Gulf of Mirabéllo seen from the hills above Ístron Bay.*

knives, pots, bronze tools and other artefacts found here it's clear that Gourniá was a thriving settlement. Its geographical position must have helped considerably, since it's an easy 12km (8 miles) from here to the south coast across the isthmus of **Ierápetra** – the alternative being a hazardous sea voyage around the eastern coastline.

Although the houses now stand only to shoulder height, most once had a second floor reached by wooden or stone stairways. The rooms may look small, but that's largely because those you see were mostly in the basements of houses. At the top of the site is a large courtyard with the palace quarters on the north side and a small shrine nearby where several cult objects (such as terracotta goddesses and snake totems) have been unearthed.

## Móhlos *

Beyond Gourniá, you pass a panoramic viewpoint at **Plátanos** before arriving at the village of **Sfáka**, 40km (25 miles) from Áyios Nikólaos, where a sharp left turn through the village is signposted to Móhlos, 6km (4 miles) away.

### PSÍRA ISLAND

Just offshore from **Móhlos** is the small islet of Psíra: you can swim to it or get one of the local fishermen to ferry you across. There's a tiny whitewashed chapel on the south side. The island – which was once attached to the mainland by a causeway – was an important Minoan settlement and the most significant finds here have come from tombs cut into the cliff-face on the west side, where magnificent jewellery, sealstones and stone vases were discovered in 1908. Excavations continue to this day.

Móhlos is a tiny seaside fishing community with just a couple of small hotels, a handful of rooms to rent, and two or three tavernas overlooking the sea. It's a peaceful, laid-back little community (despite the large package hotel further round the bay) where the main activities are lazing around in the tavernas or sunbathing on the rocks. A few small fishing-boats pull in sufficient lobster, fish and other seafood to keep visitors happy. The best taverna is on a shingle beach five minutes' walk west of the village.

### Sitía **

Crete's easternmost port, Sitía makes a good base for exploring the far eastern corner of the island. Far quieter than resort centres elsewhere, Sitía has an atmosphere all of its own which many people find compelling: in the alleyways and back streets of the town life goes on regardless, with old-fashioned cobblers' and barbers' shops rubbing shoulders with carpentry and metal workshops and agricultural supply stores serving the surrounding district.

*Steep stone steps lead up between the houses clustered on the hillsides around the old port of Sitía.*

Forming an L-shape around the harbour, the town rises up in tiers of whitewashed houses on the hillsides above the **Bay of Sitía**. The focal point of the town is the **Platía Venizélou** in the corner of the harbour, with the seafront promenade on either side packed with outdoor tavernas with views over the bay.

There are good views of the harbour from the **Venetian Fort** at the top of the northernmost part of town: almost completely destroyed on three different occasions by the Turks, the fort has been partly restored and is now used for open-air performances in the summer; you can walk around the outside but the interior is usually closed. Walking back down Kondhiláki you'll come to the **Folklore Museum** (open 10:00–12:30 weekdays in summer only, closed at weekends) which has a wonderful collection of old household implements and looms.

Many of the finds from the palace at **Káto Zákros** (see pages 78–79) are contained in the **Archaeological Museum** (open daily 08:00–14:30, closed Monday, tel: 0843-23917). The light, airy interior holds some important finds, in particular some rare Linear A tablets and a Minoan wine press. The Roman *amphorae* in the last section, which were found in a wreck, have been cunningly preserved by being displayed in a tank of sea-water!

### Moní Tóplou *

Leaving Sitía, after 12km (8 miles) the road to Palékastro passes a turning to this monastery, 3.5km (2 miles) to the left. Standing in the middle of the barren, rocky uplands, this powerful-looking building resembles nothing less than a fortress – and indeed it was a centre of resistance against invaders for several centuries.

The Moní Tóplou is one of the wealthiest and most influential monasteries on Crete, and is said to own most of the northeast corner of the island. The interior (open 09:00–13:00 and 13:15–17:00 daily) houses an important collection of reliquaries and icons, dating from the 15th to the 18th centuries. The most impressive is an extraordinary painting entitled *Lord, Thou Art Great* by Ioánnis Kornáros, with 61 minute, detailed

> ### THE ARMED MONASTERY
>
> Founded in the 14th century, Moní Tóplou was attacked by pirates in the 15th century, plundered by the Knights of St John of Malta in 1530, and sacked again by the Turks in 1646. It was the Turks who gave the monastery its present name: *touplou* is Turkish for 'with a cannon'. During World War II it was a centre for the Cretan resistance and an underground radio transmitter operated from inside the monastery (for which the Abbot was executed).

*The Archaeological Museum in Sitía contains many of the finds from the palace of Káto Zákros, including this* **larnax**, *or Minoan clay coffin.*

*The palm-forest behind the beach at Vái, said to be the only indigenous date palms in Europe.*

scenes, each inspired by a phrase from the prayer of the same name. Although unlabelled, this work is unmistakable (it's between two aisles in the main body of the chapel).

As well as the icon displays inside the chapel, a new gallery houses engravings and old books related to Greek Orthodoxy: it's a valuable collection, but probably rather dull stuff unless you're a student of religious art. A small gallery to one side houses ancient weapons from the Greek War of Independence in 1821, and some World War II firearms.

### Vái Beach ★

Undoubtedly the most over-hyped, over-visited, and over-photographed beach in Crete, with hundreds of people pouring in every day from all over the island by coach, car and motorbike for a glimpse of 'the Caribbean in the Mediterranean', Vái is famous for the palm trees which fringe its sandy beach, a strange contrast to the rocky backdrop of most Cretan beaches.

First 'discovered' by hippies, the palm tree beach was a popular camping area until the authorities discovered what was going on and the whole lot was fenced off and

declared a scientific reserve of international importance. Most of the reserve, which stretches back up a small valley from the beach, is out of bounds (although you can photograph it from the road). There's access to the beach (open 07:00–21:00 daily) from a large car park, and once on the beach sunbeds can be hired and there are facilities such as showers, toilets, a café and a restaurant.

Back at the junction with the main road there's a **Banana Plantation** (open daily except Sunday) where guided tours include all the bananas you can eat, straight from the trees. Donkey rides are also available.

### Other Nearby Beaches

A short drive north of Vái brings you to the relatively isolated beach at **Ítanos**, where there are several small sandy bays to unwind on away from the crowds. As a bonus, there's also a **Minoan city** by the entrance to the main beach. Ítanos was one of the most influential ruling cities on the eastern end of the island, flourishing from early Minoan times through the Greek and Roman eras and up to the early Byzantine period. There are traces of a basilica, and Greek walls, but it's hard to decipher much amongst the crumbled houses on the hillside.

Heading back towards Palékastro there are several other beaches signposted down rough tracks off the main road, notably **Maridati Beach** and the more accessible **Kouremenos Beach** which is said to be good for windsurfing.

### Palékastro

Palékastro is a typical farming town, with its inhabitants mostly dependent on the extensive olive groves which line the road for a considerable distance in each direction. However, its proximity to Vái, Káto Zákros and other nearby attractions means that tourism is beginning to take over, and as well as a Tourist Information Office there are also several 'pubs' and even a nightclub.

From Palékastro a road heads off left down past the hamlet of **Angathiá** (now also becoming a popular hideaway spot with rooms to rent) and continues to sandy

---

**UNSPOILED HIDEAWAY**

If you can manage it, it's best to visit **Vái** at the beginning or the end of the day when the crowds are less oppressive. Alternatively, once you've had a good look at the viewpoint at the southern end of the beach and five minutes further on there's a lovely, unspoilt sandy beach with dunes reaching back from the sea.

## A SWIFT END

One reason the **Palace of Zákros** was so rich in artefacts of all kinds is that the palace met its end very swiftly, with the inhabitants abandoning everything to escape – although quite what they were fleeing from has never been properly resolved. Some archaeologists maintain that the settlement (together with other Minoan sites) was flattened by the explosion of **Théra** (Santorini) but others disagree, believing instead that it was razed to the ground by an unspecified enemy.

*Káto Zákros is the perfect, get-away-from-it-all retreat.*

**Hiona Beach** where there are a couple of tavernas. On the right-hand side of the beach is the **archaeological site of Palékastro**, and although much of it has been filled in again to protect it from the elements you can still make out parts of the main street, stairways and dwellings.

### Káto Zákros ✶✶✶

The road from Palékastro winds lazily for 20km (12 miles) over the mountains past several semi-deserted hamlets until it arrives at **Zákros**, where a handful of tavernas depend on passing trade heading for the more compelling destination of **Káto Zákros** down on the coast.

Káto Zákros is a gem of a place, worthy of a trip in its own right even if it didn't also have a Minoan palace to boast of. At the end of a long, empty beach there are several shady tavernas, a few rooms to rent, and a handful of fishing boats – perfect relaxation away from the world.

A few paces behind the beach is the **Palace of Zákros** (open 08:00–14:30 daily, in summer until 21:00, tel: 0843-93207). One of the most interesting of Crete's Minoan sites, it has yielded a huge number of valuable treasures

when it was destroyed. British archaeologists first excavated here at the beginning of the 20th century but they missed the palace by just a few metres; it wasn't until the 1960s, when a local landowner discovered some jewellery, that excavations began in earnest.

*Simple beach-side tavernas are one of the attractions of Káto Zákros.*

Zákros is the smallest of the four Minoan palaces and this is one reason why visitors find it so attractive – it's much easier to grasp the essence of an ancient site such as this when it's compact and clearly laid out around you. Another important factor is that there's just one palace here, so you're saved the confusion of having to decipher the many different levels of excavations usually found at Minoan sites.

Zákros dates from between 1600 and 1450 BC, and in its heyday it was a major centre for trade with Egypt and Asia Minor. Its port, which is somewhere beneath the present sea-level, has never been located.

As you enter the site you'll find yourself walking down what used to be the main road to the port, with the palace on your left-hand side. The first thing you'll see is a large canopy, which shades a depression in the ground with channels leading off it – this is thought to be a **metal-smelting oven**, one of the oldest in the world.

Entering the palace, steps lead down to an inner courtyard, with the **main courtyard** and the base of an altar to the west. Beyond is the west wing, with a **ceremonial hall**, **banqueting hall**, **treasury**, and **central shrine**. In the east wing are found the **royal apartments**, with a rectangular cistern surrounded by colonnades next door which, it is thought, may have been the royal **swimming-pool**. The north wing contains a **kitchen** (the only one discovered in a Minoan palace), whilst the south wing mostly housed workshops.

> ### THE VALLEY OF THE DEAD
>
> There's an enjoyable walk from the clifftops above **Káto Zákros** down to the beach through what is known as the Valley of the Dead – so-called because the Minoans used to bury their dead in the caves along the ravine. Far from being spooky, however, the little ravine is very quiet and peaceful and, in springtime, alive with flowering plants. It takes about an hour and a half to reach the bottom of the ravine, which opens out into olive groves and banana plantations just above the Palace of Zákros. You'll need someone with transport to pick you up at the bottom, or you can catch the bus back up again.

**ISLAND ESCAPE**

One of the most popular day trips from Ierápetra is to a small island 10km (6 miles) offshore called **Gaidouronísi** (also known variously as Chrissi Island or Donkey Island). The uninhabited island is partly covered in forests of twisted trees (which the Cretans call cedars, although in fact they are a variety of sea juniper) with miles of empty beaches and sand dunes where you can laze the day away. There are a couple of tavernas. Regular caique trips run from the quayside in town throughout the season.

## Ierápetra *

This large, sprawling town – the biggest on Crete's southern coast – seems to evoke extreme reactions in those who visit it: 'Charmless and ugly, well past its sell-by-date,' claim some guidebooks, whilst others see it as 'this bright jewelled crown on the Libyan Sea' whose venerable history (stretching back some 3500 years) merits serious consideration.

Either way, Ierápetra continues to flourish, with a lively promenade along the seafront lined with competing bars and tavernas and enough space on the town's beaches to prevent them ever seeming crowded. There's nothing too demanding in the way of sightseeing, and most people seem content to while away the days moving from beach to taverna and back again until the sun goes down. The town has an enviable sunshine record, being the most southerly resort in Europe, so if it's a tan you're after you won't be disappointed: 'winter' here lasts for just two months!

There was probably a port here in Minoan times, but Ierápetra achieved its apogee under the Dorians, when it commanded more territory than any other city in Crete. It was one of the last strongholds to fall to the Romans, and under their rule it prospered as a trading centre. Many temples, theatres and other impressive buildings were erected, but little remains of them today.

Minoan finds from nearby sites are displayed in the **Archaeological Museum** (open 08:00–14:30, closed Monday) on Adriánou. If you've had your fill of Minoan artefacts by now you won't find the displays here take a great deal of energy to absorb – largely because there are no labels at all, so very little thought is required to peruse the exhibits! It's still worth a look in, if only for the beautiful **statue of Demeter** (the fertility goddess) at the end of the museum hall, which was found by a farmer ploughing his fields. Dating from around the 1st century BC, Demeter has a small altar on top of her head, with snakes entwined around it – symbols of her divinity. Another piece worth a close look is a Minoan *larnax*, or clay coffin, decorated with paintings of hunting

*This attractive Turkish fountain house stands beside the mosque in Ierápetra's old quarter.*

scenes, which can be found in the second-to-last section on the right-hand side.

The Venetians also left their mark on the city, with a **fort** (open 09:00–21:00 daily) at the end of the harbour which has recently been restored. Just behind the fort is Ierápetra's most important church, the **Panayitsa**, a single-aisled chapel containing several remarkable icons. Slightly to the west, another church, the **Aféndis Hristós**, also contains a number of fine icons and a beautifully carved wooden *iconostasis*.

Wandering back into the old Turkish quarter from the harbour you'll come across a typical old mosque, the **Tzami**, which has also recently been restored and is now used for concerts and other performances: on its west side is a small **Ottoman fountain house**.

### NAPOLEON'S HOUSE

Whilst on his way to Egypt in 1798 Napoleon moored his fleet off Ierápetra and, according to local historians, spent the night in a small house in the back streets of the Turkish quarter at 9 Káto Mera. This lovely old house, with its carved wooden door, has now been restored and is used by the Ministry of Culture to house archaeologists working on nearby sites. Evidently the archaeologists have got fed up with people wanting to look round, because a notice pinned to the wall now proclaims: 'There is nothing inside related to Napoleon – please do not disturb!'

# Eastern Crete at a Glance

## GETTING THERE

**Áyios Nikólaos** is 69km (43 miles) from Iráklion along the New Road, 60–90 min by hire car or taxi. Buses run every half hour from 06:30–21:30, and take around 90 minutes. **Eloúndha** is 20 min further on, with regular bus services to/from Áyios Nikólaos. Transfers to **Ierápetra** take 2hr 30min, with at least eight buses daily to/from Iráklion.

**Ferries** run to/from the Dodecanese direct to Áyios Nikólaos twice-weekly, and to/from the Cyclades once weekly, in summer; services are less frequent in winter.

## GETTING AROUND

**Áyios Nikólaos** is small enough to get around without a car. Most other areas in eastern Crete can be reached on public transport from Áyios Nikólaos, Eloúndha, Sitía and Ierápetra.

**Car hire** firms include: **Economy Car Hire**, 15 Akti Koundoúrou, Áyios Nikólaos, tel (0841) 22965; **Hertz**, 17 Akti Koundoúrou, Áyios Nikólaos, tel (0841) 28311 *and* 4 Pl Nikolau, Ierápetra, tel (0842) 23650.

## WHERE TO STAY

### Áyios Nikólaos

It can be extremely difficult to find a room in high season, and you'd be well advised to make an advance reservation.

*Luxury*

**Hotel St Nicolas Bay**, PO Box 47, Áyios Nikólaos 72100, tel (0841) 25041, fax (0841) 24556. 128 bungalows and suites. Within walking distance of town with its own small beach, three swimming-pools, watersports and all the usual facilities. (Deluxe)

**Minos Beach**, Áyios Nikólaos 72100, tel (0841) 22345, fax (0841) 23816. 132 rooms, 65 waterfront bungalows. Just a short walk from town with a reputation for good service and unobtrusive luxury. Heated outdoor pool, tennis, watersports. (Deluxe)

**Minos Palace**, Áyios Nikólaos 72100, tel (0841) 23801, fax (0841) 23816. 145 rooms and 7 bungalows. On the same promontory as the St Nicolas Bay, tennis, pool, watersports. (Deluxe)

*Mid-range*

**Hotel Coral**, Akti Koundoúrou, Áyios Nikólaos 72100, tel (0841) 28253, fax (0841) 28754. Well situated on the seafront. Salt-water pool on the 3rd floor terrace. Most rooms are sea-facing. (B)

**Hotel Hermes**, Akti Koundoúrou, Áyios Nikólaos 72100, tel (0841) 28253, fax (0841) 28754. Sister hotel to the Coral, just next door, with similar facilities and slightly superior rooms. (A)

**Candia Park Village**, Áyios Nikólaos 72100, tel (0841) 26811, fax (0841) 22367. Mid-way between Ag Nik and Eloúndha, this large complex of Cretan-type bungalows has two pools, aquapark, kids' mini-club, and several bars and restaurants. A good choice for families. (A)

**Odysseas**, 7 Sarolidi St, Áyios Nikólaos 72100, tel (0841) 28440. Small, family-run hotel with 24 rooms, most with *en suite* facilities and balconies with sea views. (B)

### Eloúndha

*Luxury*

**Eloúndha Beach Hotel**, Áyios Nikólaos 72100, tel (0841) 41412, fax (0841) 41373. Set in 8ha (20 acres) of landscaped gardens on the outskirts of Eloúndha, with bungalows in 'traditional' Cretan style. The facilities and service are superb. (Deluxe)

**Eloúndha Bay Hotel**, Áyios Nikólaos 72100, tel (0841) 41502, fax (0841) 41783. Formerly the Eloúndha Mare, now under the same management as the Eloúndha Beach next door. With its own private beach and top facilities throughout. (Deluxe)

*Mid-range*

**Eloúndha Marmin Hotel**, Áyios Nikólaos 72100, tel (0841) 41003. Not quite as smart as its neighbours (see above), but in a good location near the beach, in peaceful surroundings. (A)

*Budget*

**Aristea**, Áyios Nikólaos 72100, tel (0841) 41300, fax 41302. Modern hotel with good views of the harbour from the front rooms. (C)

### Istron Bay

*Luxury*

**Istron Bay Hotel**, Áyios Nikólaos 72100, tel (0841)

## Eastern Crete at a Glance

61303, fax (0841) 61383.
Extremely comfortable hotel
with a long-standing reputation, on its own private beach
13km (8 miles) to the east of
Ag Nik on the Bay of
Mirabéllo. (Deluxe)
### Móhlos
**Hotel Móhlos**, tel (0843)
94205. Family-run hotel down
a side street; the new exten-
sion has the best rooms, all
with *en suite* facilities and
large sea-facing balconies. (C)
### Sitía
**Krystal**, Kapetan Si Fi 17, Sitía
72300, tel (0841) 28484, fax
28644. Close to the seafront,
clean and comfortable, friendly management. (C)
**Elysee**, 14 K. Karamanli St,
tel (0843) 22312, fax (0843)
23427. Also on the seafront,
standard rooms but reasonably priced. (C)
### Ierápetra
**Astron**, 56 Kothri, Ierápetra
72200, tel (0842) 25114, fax
(0842) 25917. Comfortable,
well-designed hotel just next
to the beach; most of the 70
rooms have large, sea-facing
balconies. (B)
**El Greco**, 42 M. Kothri St,
Ierápetra 72200, tel (0842)
28471. Right in the centre of
town, basic rooms but good
views from those at the front.
(C)
**Cretan Villa**, 16 Lakerda St,
Ierápetra 72200, tel (0842)
28522. Exceptional rooms in
an ancient house tucked away
down a back street. Pricey,
but well worth it for the
atmosphere. (C)

### WHERE TO EAT

#### Áyios Nikólaos
**Armida Boat Club**, tel (0841)
25189. Reconstructed on the
hull of a 1920s cargo boat, a
great place for a pre- or
*après*-dinner drink (or a
liqueur coffee). On the west
side of the harbour.
**Cretan Restaurant**, Soukeras
Vassilis, tel (0841) 28773.
Overlooking the eastern side
of the harbour, sophisticated
restaurant crowded out with
plants and artefacts, international and local dishes.
**Itanos**, Platía Venizélou. Still
holding on to its reputation as
'the only genuine taverna' in
Áyios Nikólaos.
**Restaurant Hataeh**, 23
Lasíthiou St, tel (0841) 24610.
At the top of the hill, just to
the right of the hospital. A
stiff walk up from the port,
but well worth it for this
unpretentious taverna serving
traditional Greek food at
modest prices. Grilled fish a
speciality. Friendly atmosphere, excellent value.
**Fish Taverna Pelagos**, cnr of
Koraka and Katehaki, tel
(0841) 25737. Atmospheric
old building with a large
courtyard, 2 minutes from the
harbour. Excellent fish and
seafood.

#### Eloúndha
**Poulis**, tel (0841) 41451.
International and seafood,
particularly recommended for
the latter. On the seafront.
#### Sitía
**Paragadi**, 8 Karamanli St, tel
(0843) 28759. Excellent fish
dishes and traditional Greek
food.

### TOURS AND EXCURSIONS

Day trips are available from
**Áyios Nikólaos** to all the
major tourist sites on Crete.
Recommended tour operators
include: **Economy Tourline**,
15 Akti Kondoúrou St, tel
(0841) 28988; **Creta Travel
Bureau**, Sofokli Venizélou St,
tel (0841) 28496, fax 23879;
and **Adamis Tours**, tel (0841)
22770. Boat trips to
**Spinalónga** are available
through **Buzz Travel**, tel
(0841) 22608 and **Nostos
Tours**, tel (0841) 22819, fax
25336, amongst others.

### USEFUL CONTACTS

**Tourist Office**, Odhós
Paleológou, Áyios Nikólaos, tel
(0841) 22357, fax 26398. The
office is just beside the bridge
across to Lake Voulisméni.
Open 08:30–22:30.
**Tourist Police**, tel (0841)
26900.

| ÁYIOS NIKÓLAOS | J | F | M | A | M | J | J | A | S | O | N | D |
|---|---|---|---|---|---|---|---|---|---|---|---|---|
| AVERAGE TEMP. °F | 48 | 48 | 52 | 59 | 66 | 73 | 77 | 77 | 72 | 64 | 57 | 52 |
| AVERAGE TEMP. °C | 9 | 9 | 11 | 15 | 12 | 23 | 25 | 25 | 22 | 18 | 14 | 11 |
| Hours of Sun Daily | 5 | 5 | 6 | 7 | 10 | 12 | 10 | 10 | 9 | 7 | 5 | 5 |
| RAINFALL " | 3 | 2 | 1 | 1 | 0.5 | 0.5 | 0 | 0 | 0.5 | 1 | 2 | 4 |
| RAINFALL mm | 78 | 47 | 36 | 26 | 9 | 9 | 2 | 0 | 12 | 34 | 102 | 102 |
| Days of Rainfall | 8 | 8 | 7 | 4 | 2 | 1 | 0 | 0 | 1 | 4 | 10 | 10 |

# 5
# Réthimnon Province

**M**ore than any other province, Réthimnon is dominated by mountain ranges. To the east, it is
hemmed in by Crete's highest peaks in the Psilorítis
Massif, whilst to the west the craggy peaks of the Lefká
Óri (the White Mountains) form the boundary with western Crete. Between these two ranges are numerous high
valleys, carpeted with wild flowers in spring, where
sleepy villages seem almost cut off from the world.

The north coast is bordered by a flat, coastal plain
leading down to long sandy beaches with a considerable
number of resort hotels and unattractive developments.
By contrast, the charming provincial capital of
**Réthimnon** inspires great affection from its devotees,
with old Venetian and Turkish buildings embellishing its
attractive historic centre and harbour.

The south coast is punctuated by massive headlands
with secluded bays tucked away at the end of long,
winding roads. The most popular base on this coast is
the fast-expanding resort of **Ayía Galíni**, which buzzes
with activity day and night. Further to the west **Plakiás**
is another busy tourist centre. Between the two is the
famous **Palm Beach**, an oddity similar to Vái Beach (see
page 76) which attracts day-trippers by the score.

There are hardly any Minoan sites in this part of
Crete (at least, few have been discovered) but there are
several interesting monasteries, most notably **Moní
Arkádhi** and **Moní Préveli**, both of which have served
as centres of resistance in a province where the people
are renowned for their fiercely independent spirit.

**DON'T MISS**

\*\*\* Wandering around the
old streets in **Réthimnon**.
\*\* Dinner on the **harbour-
side** in **Réthimnon**.
\*\*\* A visit to the **Monastery
of Arkádhi**.
\*\* An evening bar-hopping
in **Ayía Galíni**.
\* Mountain villages in the
**Amári Valley**.
\* Bargaining for weavings in
**Anóyia**.

**Opposite:** *The lovely old
balconied houses around
the harbour in Réthimnon
are now nearly all
restaurants, with tables
crowding the waterfront.*

*The entrance to Réthimnon's huge Fortezza, designed as an impregnable protection for the inhabitants of the town, but simply by-passed by the invading Turks.*

### Réthimnon ✱✱✱

Réthimnon is one of the most delightful towns in Crete, rivalled only by Hanía for the atmosphere of the picturesque back streets around its harbour area. You would hardly realize it when arriving by road through the outer suburbs – which are a sprawling mass of concrete buildings – but the town's central core, complete with ancient Turkish houses and minarets, nestles like a pearl in its ugly outer shell.

Apart from the harbour, the focal point of the town for most visitors is the long, sandy **beach** which stretches away eastwards from the centre. It's backed up by a busy promenade lined with restaurants, car hire offices, and small hotels, with most of the bigger hotels towards the eastern end. The most sheltered area of the beach is right next to the harbour, but it is less crowded past the breakwaters to the east, where the water is also cleaner.

The **harbour** itself was built by the Venetians but is prone to silting up, so it is used only by small craft such as caiques and fishing boats (the Piraeus ferry has to dock on the seaward side of the harbour walls). It is surrounded by lovely old Italianate houses with wrought iron balconies and wooden shutters – nowadays almost every single one of these is a restaurant, with tables laid out right up to the water's edge: the setting is such that prices tend to be on the high side but it's a great place for a special night out.

Away from the beach and the harbour, Réthimnon's chief delight is in simply wandering around the back streets and narrow alleys, where the Turks left their mark in the form of beautiful, ornate wooden balconies projecting from the first floors of many houses. Ornate Venetian stonework and several Turkish fountains tucked away in odd corners add interest to the atmospheric old quarter. There are plenty of unusual little shops and tempting restaurants and cafés throughout this area.

There are several landmarks worth watching out for here, such as the **Rimondi Fountain** on Platía Petiháki; built by the Venetian Governor of Réthimnon in 1629 (supposedly because he was envious of the Morosini

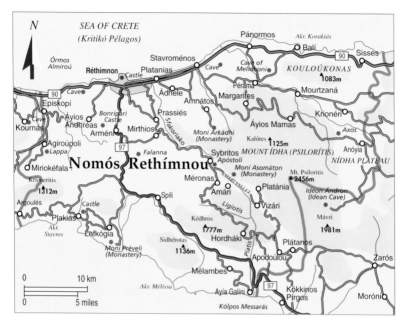

Fountain in Iráklion), it sports three lions with bulging eyes who still spout water from their mouths into a marble bowl. Just down Paleológou from here is the Venetian **Loggia**, until recently the home of the archaeological museum but now undergoing conversion into a library. Also nearby is the **Nerandzes Mosque**, with its three bulging domes and soaring minaret; there are terrific views of the town from the top of the minaret but, sadly, the stonework is deteriorating and the stairway to the top is now closed indefinitely.

Continuing up the central street of Ethníkis Andistásis will bring you to the **Porta Guora**, which was once the main gateway to the town. Opposite the gate are the **Public Gardens**, rather tatty but worth visiting if there is an outdoor play or concert.

Another Venetian legacy is the impressive **Fortezza** which dominates a small peninsula on the west side of the town. Walking around its massive ramparts and bastions it's easy to believe the claim that this was the

---

**THE REDUNDANT FORT**

Réthimnon's massive **Fortezza** was designed to house the entire population of the town in the event of an attack – a function it was clearly capable of fulfilling given its sheer size. However, the fort turned out to be a white elephant. The first time it was put to the test was when the Turks attacked in 1645, but the invaders simply bypassed the fort and captured the town in less than 24 hours.

## ROUTES TO THE SOUTH

There are two routes to the south coast from Réthimnon:
• The **westerly** route climbs rapidly up into the mountains and passes **Arméni**; 20km (12 miles) from Réthimnon is the first right turn for Plakiás, leading down through the **Kotsifoú Gorge**. The second turn-off descends via the **Kourtaliótiko Gorge** – both are fairly spectacular.
• The **easterly** route is the slower of the two, traversing the remote **Amári Valley**. The distance to Ayia Galíni is about the same – around 65km (40 miles).

largest Venetian fortress ever built. Its main purpose was to protect the town from a series of pirate raids in the late 16th century but its usefulness, alas, was short-lived. Entering the interior (open 08:00–20:00 in summer, 08:00–19:00 in winter) you'll discover some fine views over the coastline and the town: the huge open space inside the walls is scattered with various ruins (such as those of the barrack houses and an ingenious set of cisterns for collecting rainwater) as well as an enormous mosque (now restored) and an open-air theatre.

Opposite the entrance to the Fortezza is the **Archaeological Museum** (open 08:00–14:30, closed Monday), now housed inside an old converted prison. Exhibits from the surrounding area include Neolithic finds, Minoan pottery, and an interesting collection of Greek and Roman coins.

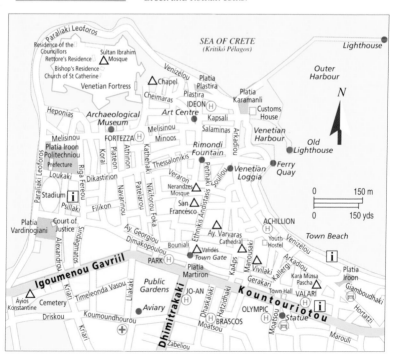

*The Moní Arkádhi, a focal point of Cretan resistance against the Turks in the 19th century.*

### Moní Arkádhi ★★★

Set on a small plateau within the foothills of the Psilorítis Range, the Monastery of Arkádhi is easily reached on a day trip from Réthimnon, 25km (16 miles) to the north-west. It's a journey well worth making since, although the monastery holds no great art works or anything of that kind, it has an atmosphere all of its own which is largely due to its heroic role in the Cretan fight for freedom from the Turkish yoke in the 19th century.

During the 1866 uprising against the Turks the monastery became a focal point for resistance fighters all over the island. Hundreds of men, women and children perished here on 9 November rather than let the monastery fall into Turkish hands, a gesture which came to symbolize Cretan courage in the face of the invaders. This mass suicide shocked the world and aroused widespread sympathy for the Cretan cause, but it wasn't for another 30 years that the island was finally free from the Turks.

The roofless **powder magazine** is on the north side of the monastery compound, just in front of the refectory where the few survivors of the blast were butchered. In the middle of the quadrangle is the impressive **church** which was built in 1587 (its richly decorated façade appears on the 100 drachma note). On the south side, a small **museum** (open 09:00–18:00 daily) contains various liturgical mementoes and blood-stained clothing from the carnage.

---

**THE GUNPOWDER PLOT**

As the Turks advanced through the province in 1866, people from Réthimnon and its surroundings fled to the **Arkádhi Monastery** to join the resistance fighters: 325 men and 639 women and children were inside the monastery on 7 November, surrounded by 5000 Turkish troops. Despite the hopeless odds the defenders battled on through the day of 8 November, and many died on both sides. During the night they realized it was only a matter of time before they would be overwhelmed, and hatched a plan to go out in a blaze of glory by blowing up the powder magazine. Thus it was that on 9 November, as the Turks battered their way through the west gate of the monastery, the survivors gathered in the powder magazine and the abbot gave the signal to ignite the gunpowder. The resulting blast killed most of those inside, but they managed to take dozens of Turks with them.

### THE CHARCOAL BURNERS

Alongside the road from
Pérama to Melidóni you'll see
numerous blackened heaps
which are the work of local
charcoal burners. In the summer months they can be seen
sawing up cypresses and
other old trees to create huge
mounds which burn down
slowly to form the charcoal.
This old skill still exists thanks
to the huge demand from
tourists for chargrilled fish
and *souvláki*.

## Balí **

Travelling eastwards from Réthimnon the coastal plain
terminates abruptly at **Pánormos** and from here to
Iráklion the road dips and swoops around the steep
headlands beneath the Kouloúkonas Range. Hidden
away around 2km (1 mile) off the New Road is the resort
of Balí, spreading itself over several tiny coves beneath
the thorn and *phrígana*-covered hillsides.

Once a tranquil fishing village, Balí is now firmly on
the tourist map and there are numerous apartment
blocks and hotels amidst its white-painted houses and
tavernas.

Approaching from the main road, the first beach you
come to is **Camper's Beach** (as the name implies, there's
a campsite here), followed by **Greystone Beach** (which is
not particularly inviting) and then **Balí Beach**, site of the
luxurious Balí Beach Hotel. Past here, the old village is
clustered around **Harbour Beach**, with the last one (variously known as **Paradise Beach** or **Evita Beach**) accessible by a short walk over the headland. This is by far the
best of the beaches here, a sandy little cove with a small
rocky outcrop a few metres offshore for sunbathing and
diving from.

Balí offers a good selection of watersports (including
water-skiing, pedalos and canoes) and a lively nightlife.
It does get fairly crowded in high season, however.

*Charcoal burning is an
ancient skill which is still
practised in several parts
of Crete.*

## The Melidóni Cave

Inland from the coast, the large agricultural town of **Pérama** is the access point for the **Melidóni Cave**, another shrine to Cretan heroism in a region which seems positively littered with them.

A short drive or walk outside the village of Melidóni, 5km (3 miles) from Pérama, the cave is adorned with stalactites and stalagmites and is said to have been occupied since Neolithic times. Its notoriety, however, derives from the Turkish occupation, when around 300 villagers sought refuge inside the cave in 1824: the Turkish commander ordered them out but when they refused (and shot his messengers), he blocked up the entrance in an attempt to suffocate them. The villagers simply made new air-holes, so the Turks piled up branches and other combustible material in front of the cave and set it on fire: all those inside perished from asphyxiation. A shrine in the first chamber commemorates those poor souls.

## Anóyia *

The largest mountain village in Crete, Anóyia is famed for its weaving and sheep's wool rugs. Surrounded by high mountain pastures, it is the main centre of goat and sheep rearing on the island. But the large number of weaving looms in the village is also due to the bitter recent history of Anóyia which left it with few menfolk – and dozens of widows who were forced to turn their hand to weaving to make a living.

Anóyia has long had a reputation for music and folk dancing, and once tourism arrived on Crete it quickly became a focus for 'Cretan nights'. This, along with the sale of weavings, forms the mainstay of the village economy today.

The village itself is not particularly attractive and, indeed, some of the textiles on display are of dubious quality. However, Anóyia is in a superb setting, surrounded by mountain ridges, and it makes an interesting excursion from the coast. The road from Anóyia circles the Nídha Plateau to reach the Idean Cave (see page 93).

### VILLAGE MASSACRE

During World War II, when the resistance fighters captured the commander-in-chief of the German forces, **General Kreipe**, Anóyia was one of the villages where he was hidden before being abducted from the island. In retaliation, the Germans entered the village on 15 August 1944, destroyed every building except the church and then killed every male they could find.

## ZEUS AGAIN

Although the honour of being the birthplace of Zeus is also claimed by the **Dhiktean Cave** (see page 71), mythologists agree that at the very least he was brought up in the **Idean Cave**. It became a centre of pilgrimage from Minoan times onwards, and was even visited by Pythagoras in later years.

## Mount Psilorítis **

The Psilorítis Range dominates the eastern half of Réthimnon Province, with its lofty peak, **Mount Psilorítis**, rising up from the roof of Crete to 2456m (8057ft) – the highest point on the island.

Conquering Mount Psilorítis (also known as Mount Ídha) is the goal of every serious hiker who visits Crete, and the round trip to the summit can be accomplished in around eight hours. This isn't a climb that should be attempted on your own, however, and it is advisable to hire a guide.

Even if you're not planning to climb Psilorítis the journey by car part of the way up the mountain is still

*The Psilorítis Range forms the backbone of Réthimnon Province: high up on the slopes of Mount Psiloritítis is the Idean Cave, where legend has it that Zeus spent his childhood.*

worth doing. The easiest access is from **Anóyia**, whence it is a 20km (12 mile) drive to the start of the **Nídha Plateau**. This small plateau, nearly 1400m (4600ft) above sea-level, is used as summer pasture for large flocks of sheep and goats; scattered about the plain are numerous little stone huts, known as *mitáta*, in which the shepherds traditionally make cheeses and yoghurt. As the snows melt in the spring, the plateau blazes with wild flowers such as crocus and chionodoxa.

The road loops around the western edge of the plain and finishes by a modern taverna (now closed and used only by private climbing groups). From here it is a 20-minute walk up to the entrance of the **Idean Cave** (**Idéon Ándron**). According to legend, this is where Zeus was born; excavations inside the cave began in 1885, and several gold and ivory objects uncovered here are now on display in the Iráklion Museum (Room XII).

The current excavations have been going on for a decade or more, but unfortunately the extent of the digging means that the cave may well still be closed to the public.

## The Amári Valley *

One of the least visited areas in this part of Crete, the Amári Valley runs between the Psilorítis Range to the east and the less daunting Kédros Range to the west. It's a wonderful area to explore at a leisurely pace, with dozens of little villages set in a verdant landscape of olive groves, vineyards and orchards. There is also a surprising number of frescoed churches, most of which survived the destruction meted out to many of the villages during the Second World War because of their role in supporting the resistance.

Good roads run down either side of the valley, which can conveniently be visited on a round trip from Ayía Galíni or on the journey between the two coasts.

From Ayía Galíni, follow the road up the eastern side of the valley to **Apodoúlou**, where you can explore a Minoan vaulted **tomb** (known as a *tholos*) on the northern outskirts of the village. Ten minutes' walk away is

*Perfect for leisurely exploration and worlds away from the busy coastal resorts, the verdant hillsides of the Amári Valley are planted with olives and vines, and dotted with isolated villages.*

the little chapel of **Áyios Geórgios**, which has a set of 14th-century frescoes.

Turn left at **Fourfourás** towards **Vizári**, where there is an early Christian **basilica** (one of the oldest on the island) 1km (half a mile) to the west of the village. From here the road runs straight across the vineyards and olive groves of the plain, leading up towards the **Moní Asomáton** (Monastery of the Assumption). The Venetian-style monastery buildings now house an agricultural college, and were once an important centre for learning on the island. You can stroll amongst the buildings, which are surrounded by orange trees, maples and even palm trees.

Backtracking briefly down a side road brings you to **Amári**, the valley's main village, from where there are superb views back across to Mount Psilorítis. In a small wood just outside the village the church of **Ayía Ánna** contains the oldest authenticated frescoes on Crete, dating from 1225.

More impressive frescoes can be found in the **Panayía** (the church) just outside **Thrónos** at the head of the valley. You can also see the much older mosaic floor (possibly dating back to the 4th century BC) upon which the church was built.

Looping back towards **Méronas** on the west side of the valley you'll pass through the main fruit-growing areas. Most of the villages on this side of the valley are comparatively modern, due to the fact that they were razed to the ground during World War II as retribution for sheltering partisans. Beside the road between Méronas and Elénes you'll come across the **Moní Áyios**

**Ioánnis Theológos**: this old ruin also houses a set of weather-beaten frescoes.

From here, the road runs round past **Yerakári** and several other mountain villages, with vistas across the valley to the Psilorítis Range.

## Ayía Galíni ★★★

Some holiday brochures claim that Ayía Galíni is still very much a fishing village, but it is hard to credit this description in high season, when the south coast's busiest resort is thronged with hundreds of people and the bars and discos are going full blast. Ayía Galíni is an unusual resort with a relaxed, easy-going atmosphere – the perfect place for a fun holiday, as long as you're not expecting the tranquillity of a *real* fishing village.

It's partly its situation that makes Ayía Galíni so appealing: nestled in a fold of the mountains, the village tumbles down the hillside and opens out into a small harbour area surrounded by inviting tavernas and restaurants. Indeed, food is one of the main reasons for coming here, with dozens of restaurants offering a huge choice of menus; some of the busiest are in the pedestrian street (predictably known as '**Taverna Row**') behind the harbour. Spreading out from Taverna Row are the resort's shops, music bars, and 'rent rooms'.

Tourism has boomed in Ayía Galíni despite its lack of a good beach – there is just one small pebble-and-sand patch to the east of the harbour and it tends to become crowded in high season. However, feasibility studies are currently under way to create a big, sandy beach here. Ayía Galíni also has a brand new, EU-financed marina, but since the south coast of Crete is not on the main Mediterranean cruising routes this may prove something of a white elephant.

## Moní Préveli ★★★

In an isolated spot high above the cliffs of the south coast, Moní Préveli (open 08:00–18:00 daily) was once one of the wealthiest monasteries on Crete. Only a handful of monks still live here, but the monastery is a popu-

---

**NEARBY BEACHES**

Whilst Ayía Galíni's beach isn't brilliant, there are several others nearby which you can reach on day trips:
• **Áyios Yióryios** is an attractive shingle cove with two tavernas behind it, reached by walking (two hours each way), car or daily boat excursions from the harbour.
• **Áyios Pávlos** is the best beach in the vicinity, a sheltered little bay to the west bordered by unusual rock formations. Accessible by car (via Mélambes) or daily boat trips from the harbour.
• You can also walk along the deserted **shoreline** to the east of Ayía Galíni, where the long, pebbly beach extends all the way to **Kókkinos Pírgos** (around 90 minutes' walk one way: you can catch the bus back).

### THE RICHES OF PRÉVELI

The monastery of Préveli acquired much of its wealth during the Turkish occupation: the fiercely independent Cretans, determined not to lose their possessions to their oppressive rulers, preferred to give them to the church. Moní Préveli controlled extensive olive groves, grazing and arable land, investing its income in churches, schools and hospitals as well as the icons, books and other treasures in its own collection.

lar place to visit largely because of its role in World War II, when the monks assisted Allied troops to escape by submarine from a nearby beach. Like other monasteries, it was also a noted centre of resistance under the Turks.

At the back of the courtyard, the 19th-century **church** contains some rich carvings, an elaborate *iconostasis* (altar wall), and the Golden Cross – said to contain a fragment from the True Cross. In front of the church, a small and somewhat claustrophobic **museum** holds relics from the past including some beautiful old silverwork such as candlesticks and censers. The courtyard, with its fountains and plane trees, enjoys superb views out to sea.

### Préveli Beach (Palm Beach) *

Below the cliffs to the east of Moní Préveli, **Palm Beach** must once have been a superb spot. The little sandy cove sits at the mouth of the **Kourtaliótiko Gorge**, where a broad stream tumbles down shallow rapids between a miniature oasis of palm trees, oleanders and eucalyptus. The river forms a small lagoon behind the beach, creating a picture-perfect scene: sadly, Palm Beach has become too popular for its own good, and is now so

*The Monastery of Préveli on the south coast sheltered Allied troops before their evacuation after the Battle of Crete, and offerings from grateful recipients of its protection can be seen in the church.*

overrun with day-trippers that the place is a mess (there are no proper rubbish disposal or toilet facilities).

There are several ways to reach Palm Beach: the easiest is by following the dirt track which branches off next to a Venetian Bridge on the main road to Moní Préveli, and then taking a shuttle-boat around the cliff. Alternatively, you can scramble down a steep track which starts from the clifftop a little to the east of Moní Préveli. There are also boat trips from Plakiás.

*Where the mountains meet the sea: the coastline of southwest Crete, near Plakiás.*

## Plakiás **

Surrounded by steep mountain peaks, the long, sweeping bay of Plakiás is one of the most attractive along the whole southern coast. The original village, with its tiny harbour, sits at the western end of a huge sandy beach shaded by tamarisk trees. Near the harbour the beach tends to be pebbly, but towards the craggy headland at the western end it becomes sandier and less crowded. The long beach is fairly exposed and windy – but this is good news for the windsurfers who take advantage of offshore breezes in the afternoons.

The village itself has become highly popular in the last few years, with buildings rising on all sides at an alarming rate, but for the moment it remains relatively relaxed and low-key. There is a growing number of bars, shops and tavernas in the village centre, and even a disco just outside on the coast road.

Plakiás is a particularly good choice in the springtime, with some lovely walks amongst the wild flowers on the mountain slopes above the village, around villages such as **Mírthios** and **Sellía**.

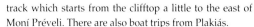

> ### FURTHER AFIELD
>
> To the east of Plakiás there are several other good beaches within easy walking distance:
> • **Damnóni Beach** is about 30 minutes' walk (via a turning off the Lefkóyia road). It has a fine sandy beach with one hotel and two tavernas.
> • **Bay of Pigs** is another beautiful little bay just past Damnóni – the name is not thought to refer to the fact that it's almost entirely nudist!
> • **Amoúdi Beach** is the next one along, a lovely cove shaded by tamarisk trees with just one taverna and good snorkelling around the rocky headlands.

## Réthimnon at a Glance

**Réthimnon** town is 78km (48 miles) from Iráklion and 59km (37 miles) from Haniá along the north coast New Road. Buses run every hour to and from Iráklion and Haniá.

**Réthimnon** has plenty of **car** and **motorbike rental** outlets, amongst them **Ideal Motion**, 58 Stamathiudaki St, tel (0831) 51062, **Car Plan**, 50 Sofia Venizélou St, tel (0831) 54825, and **Greenways**, Adelianos Kampos, tel (0831) 72274. Car and bike rentals are also available in **Balí**, **Ayía Galíni** and **Plakiás**.

The **Arkádi Monastery** can easily be visited by **bus** from Réthimnon. To reach **Balí** on public transport you'll have to take a Réthimnon-Iráklion bus, ask for the Balí stop by a Shell garage and walk the last 2km (1 mile). For **Mount Psilorítis**, the **Amári Valley**, **Moní Préveli** and **Palm Beach** you're better off with your own transport.

There are frequent buses (between six and eight daily) to **Ayía Galíni** from Iráklion and Réthimnon. **Plakiás** can be reached directly from Réthimnon (five daily buses) or via Ayía Galíni (twice daily).

*Réthimnon*
*Mid-range*
**Hotel Grecotel Rithymna**

**Beach**, tel (0831) 71002, fax (0831) 71668. Popular family resort hotel on the beach 7km (4 miles) from the centre; three pools, fitness club, water sports centre. (A)
**Hotel Orion**, tel (0831) 71471, fax (0831) 71474. On the beach 7km (4 miles) from the centre, pool, roof garden. (B)
**Mythos Suites Hotel**, 12 Karaoli Dimitriou St, Réthimnon 7410, tel (0831) 53917, fax (0831) 51036. New studio/apartment block, well-appointed rooms, pool. (B)
**Hotel Fortezza**, 16 Melisinou St, Réthimnon 7410, tel (0831) 23828, fax (0831) 54073). Convenient, central location with its own pool. (B)
**The Byzantine**, 26 Vosporou, Sq 4 Martyron, Réthimnon 7410, tel (0831) 55609). Hidden away in the back streets of the old town, this former palace has been beautifully renovated and furnished with antiques. Elegant, secluded, and highly atmospheric. (B)
**Hotel Ideon**, 10 Pl Plastíra, Réthimnon 7410, tel (0831) 28667, fax (0831) 28670. Modern building but an excellent location on the seafront in the old town; pool. (B)
*Budget*
**Seeblick**, 17 Pl Plastíra, Réthimnon 7410, tel (0831) 22478. On the seafront in the old town, reasonable value but hard to get a room in season. (C)

*Balí*
**Balí Beach Hotel**, tel (0834) 94210. Large hotel but reasonably attractive, built down a hillside to its own small beach. (C)
*Ayía Galíni*
*Mid-range*
**Irini Mare**, Ayía Galíni 74056, tel (0832) 91488, fax (0832) 91166. Superb new hotel near the beach; tasteful, spacious rooms, pool. (A)
**Andromeda**, Ayía Galíni 74056, tel (0832) 91264. Handy location at the top of the village. (C)
**Pension Stella**, Ayía Galíni 74056, tel (0832) 91357. In a peaceful spot close to the resort centre, spotless rooms, friendly management. (B)
*Budget*
**Fevro Hotel**, Ayía Galíni 74056, tel (0832) 91275, fax (0832) 91475. Small, friendly hotel near the centre. (C)
**Hotel Glaros**, Ayía Galíni 74056, tel (0832) 91151, fax 91159. Modern, well-designed hotel built back into the hillside (no lift). (C)
*Plakiás*
*Mid-range*
**New Alianthos Hotel**, Plakiás 74060, tel (0832) 31280. New hotel with spacious, bright rooms. Pool. Five minutes from the village centre. (B)
**Hotel Lamon**, Plakiás 74060, tel (0832) 31279. Just across the road from the beach, simple but attractive rooms. (C)
*Budget*
**Plakiás Bay Hotel**, Plakiás

74060, tel (0832) 31215, fax (0832) 31951. In a superb position at the western end of the bay, 28 apartments with verandahs. Attractive, welcoming little hotel. (C)
**Hotel Livykon**, Plakiás 74060, tel (0832) 31216, fax 31216. On the shore road, straightforward and reasonably priced. (C)
**Hotel Sophia**, Plakiás 74060, tel (0832) 31251, fax 31252. Reasonable budget choice just behind the village. (C)
**Secret Nest**, Plakiás 74060, tel (0832) 31235. Good value rooms and apartments above the restaurant of the same name. (C)

## WHERE TO EAT

### Réthimnon
**Seven Brothers**. On the inner harbour, but reasonably priced compared to most of the others here. Chargrilled fish a speciality.
**Palazzo**. On the inner harbour, and you can also eat on the atmospheric rooftop balcony.
**Vassilis**. If you're fed up with harbour views the interior of this old taverna makes a change – it's decorated with masses of old paintings and photos. Inner harbour.
**Alana**, 11 Salaminos. Pretty courtyard garden in the old town, extensive menu.
**Carribbean**, Platía Petiháki. Opposite Rimondi Fountain; simple food in basic but very relaxed surroundings. Live jazz Thu, Fri, Sat 20:30.

### Ayía Galini
**Rocka's**. Superb music bar overlooking the square with an outside terrace, excellent food, cocktails.
**La Strada**, tel (0832) 91262. Popular Italian restaurant with a wide range of pizzas and pasta.
**Madame Ordans**, tel (0832) 91215. In a lovely position overlooking the harbour, good value for a special night out (steaks, lobster etc).
**Incognito**, tel (0832) 91414. Lively, fun music bar in the back streets.
**The Garden of Chrysanthemums**, tel (0832) 91277. Set in a tranquil, flower-filled garden on the main square. Good food at reasonable prices.

### Plakiás
**Sunset Taverna**. On the small headland just to the west of the village, reasonable prices.
**Julia's**. Excellent selection of inventive, home-made vegetarian dishes as well as snacks, light lunches and soups.
**Christos**. Popular taverna with a large terrace shaded by tamarisk trees.
**Zorba's**, tel (0832) 31333. Seafood, pizza and pasta as well as all the usual Greek dishes.

## TOURS AND EXCURSIONS

From Réthimnon harbour there are daily cruises on the *Scorpios* eastwards towards **Pánormos** and the **Scaléta sea caves**. The *Creta Wave* operates daily westwards along the coast to **Georgioúpolis** and **Sóudha Bay**. Both boats depart from the inner harbour, where there is also a *Pirate Ship* with daily coastal cruises.
   **Guided walking tours** (small groups) in five different nearby areas are offered by **The Happy Walker**, 56 Tobazi St, Réthimnon 74100, tel/fax (0831) 52920. There is also an office for the **Mountain Climbing Bureau**, who offer trekking, mountain bike tours, and climbing. M. Portaliou 31, Réthimnon 74100, tel (0831) 55855.

## USEFUL CONTACTS

**Tourist Office**, Eleftheriou Venizélou, Réthimnon, tel (0831) 29148. On the seafront promenade. Open 08:30–15:30 Mon to Fri.
**Tourist Police**, tel (0831) 28156. In the same building as the tourist office.

| RÉTHIMNON | J | F | M | A | M | J | J | A | S | O | N | D |
|---|---|---|---|---|---|---|---|---|---|---|---|---|
| AVERAGE TEMP. °F | 59 | 61 | 63 | 68 | 75 | 82 | 86 | 86 | 81 | 75 | 70 | 63 |
| AVERAGE TEMP. °C | 15 | 16 | 17 | 20 | 24 | 28 | 30 | 30 | 27 | 24 | 21 | 17 |
| Hours of Sun Daily | 5 | 5 | 5 | 7 | 10 | 11 | 12 | 11 | 9 | 6 | 5 | 5 |
| RAINFALL * | 5 | 4 | 3 | 1 | 0.5 | 0 | 0 | 0 | 1 | 4 | 3 | 4 |
| RAINFALL mm | 138 | 94 | 78 | 37 | 12 | 6 | 1 | 2 | 21 | 90 | 72 | 110 |
| Days of Rainfall | 16 | 13 | 10 | 7 | 3 | 1 | 0 | 1 | 3 | 8 | 10 | 15 |

# 6
# Western Crete

Embracing the entire westernmost chunk of the island, the province of Haniá is one of the most spectacular and least visited areas in Crete. It has little in the way of Minoan sites but this is more than compensated for by the wild scenery, the peaceful back roads leading to charming rural villages, and hidden coves and beaches waiting to be explored.

The province's capital, the city of **Haniá**, is packed with historic buildings. The island's second largest city, it is undeniably the most attractive, and boasts the most beautiful harbour in Crete. It makes an excellent base for exploring the northern part of the province, including the nearby peninsulas of **Akrotíri** and **Rodhópou**; beyond the third (almost inaccessible) peninsula of Gramvoúsa the blunt, western coastline harbours several magnificent beaches. The most accessible of these is **Falásarna**, a delightful spot which is well worth the effort to get to. On the far southwest tip of the island, **Elafonísi** is one of those few coastal areas which was never extensively inhabited: the main attraction is simply sand and sea.

The southern half of the province is dominated by the dramatic peaks of the **Lefká Óri** (the White Mountains); their impenetrable mass makes road-building almost impossible, and many little resorts on the south coast (such as **Loutró** and **Ayía Rouméli**) can only be reached by boat – although the latter can also be reached on foot through the **Samariá Gorge**, the longest gorge in Europe and one of Crete's most popular walking excursions.

### DON'T MISS

\*\*\* Harbour and old town, **Haniá**.
\*\*\* **Falásarna** and **Elafonísi** beaches.
\*\*\* A walk through the **Samariá Gorge**.
\*\* The **Archaeological Museum**, Haniá.
\*\* A visit to **Loutró**.
\* The monasteries on the **Akrotíri Peninsula**.

**Opposite:** *The 17th-century monastery of Ayía Triádha on the Akrotíri peninsula.*

**ISLAND CAPITAL**

With the end of the Turkish occupation in 1898, Haniá was made the capital of independent Crete under the Great Powers. It remained the capital when Crete became part of Greece in 1913, and it wasn't until 1971 that it relinquished this role to the present-day capital, Iráklion. In terms of the arts and academia it still considers itself the more important centre, and houses Crete's Court of Appeal as well as the Art and Architecture faculties of the University of Crete.

### Haniá ★★★

Relaxing in a smart café on Haniá's lovely waterfront, with the Lefká Óri rising majestically above the rooftops, it's hard to imagine that the city has had such a long and turbulent history. Originally founded by Kydon (a grandson of King Minos), the settlement was called **Kydonia** in his honour. After the fall of Knossós it became the centre of Mycenaean power on the island, and continued to flourish during the Hellenistic and Roman eras. During the Venetian occupation the city was renamed **La Canea**; the Genoese briefly took control between 1266 and 1290, and on their return the Venetians proceeded to fortify the main citadel, a hill known as the **Kastélli**.

In the 16th century the threat of raids by Turkish pirates forced the Venetians to extend the fortifications

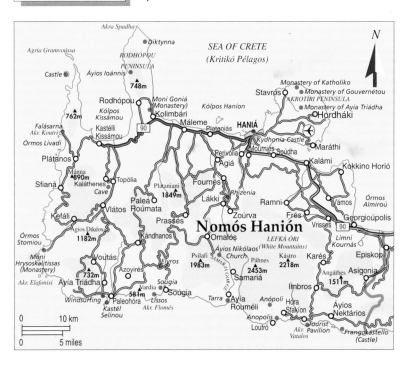

*Haniá harbour: its bustling waterfront lined with restaurants and cafés has an atmosphere which will induce you to linger.*

still further. But this proved of little use when the Turks overran the city in 1645. It became the seat of the Pasha and the island's capital, with the Turks embellishing many of the Venetian buildings to give the old town the rich architectural mix it retains today.

During World War II, Haniá was close to the scene of some of the heaviest fighting in the **Battle of Crete**, and much of the city was wiped out by bombardment and fire storms. Luckily, the older part was spared.

Once you're past the ugly outer suburbs, Haniá is a relatively easy city to find your way around. The main road from Réthimnon emerges into **Platía 1866**, a tree-shaded square which lies on the edge of the old and new parts of Haniá. The main **bus station** is just to the south, with the **Tourist Office** (NTOG) to the west of the square.

The large and unusual **covered market** is five minutes' walk to the west (down Yiánari), while directly in front of you the main thoroughfare of **Hálidhon** (stuffed full of jewellery and souvenir shops and food outlets) leads down to the harbour. Halfway down on the right-hand side a large plaza opens out onto Haniá's **Cathedral**, with the **Folk Museum** and the **Archaeological Museum** on the left-hand side.

Hálidhon opens out into a busy square bordering the harbour – not surprisingly, it's generally known as **Harbour Square** (officially, it's Platía Sindriváni). Directly across the water, the old Venetian **lighthouse** stands sentinel at the harbour entrance. To the right is

---

### SHOPPING IN HANIA

Haniá is an excellent place for shops, particularly for leather, craftwork and designer jewellery.

• If you've got money to splurge on high quality antique weavings, look in at **Kostas Liapakis**, 3 Angélou Street, who specializes in rich and elaborate **kelims** and **blankets**.

• **Odhós Theotokopoúlou** is the place to look for ceramics, exclusive jewellery and crafts. Some of the better outlets include **Para Hin Alos** (#39), **Metamorphosis** (#50), **Peritechno** (#19) and **Rodopetalo** (#24).

• Haniá's **leather alley**, **Odhós Skridhlof**, runs at right angles to Hálidhon above the cathedral. A dozen or more little shops on either side overflow with boots, bags, belts, sandals and other items.

• The **covered market** to the east of Platía 1886 is a good place to pick up picnic supplies, with masses of fresh fruit and vegetables, speciality cheese and olive stalls, and bakeries. It's also worth looking here for souvenirs to take home, such as herbs, honey or *raki*.

*The old town of Haniá with its rich mix of Turkish and Venetian architecture, invites leisurely strolls around the quiet back streets.*

the large white dome of the **Mosque of the Janissaries**, which until recently housed a branch of the tourist office but is now being restored for other purposes. Go around to the right and you'll come to the **inner harbour**, backed by a row of Venetian **arsenals**; some of these crumbling structures have been restored and now house exhibitions and other similar events in the summer.

Behind the arsenals is the **Kastélli**, a small hill which is the oldest inhabited part of the city. This is a delightful area to stroll through, with parts of old walls and stonework incorporated into charming, flower-covered house fronts.

In the opposite direction from the Kastélli the harbour wall curves round the huge semicircle of **Aktí Koundourióti**. This is Haniá's *pièce de résistance*, best seen at night when the lights from dozens of restaurants and cafés twinkle across the water and the animated *vólta* is in full force.

At the end of the long row of restaurants the ground rises towards the **Fírkas**, a squat Venetian bastion which you can wander around for views of the harbour behind. Housed in a gateway is Haniá's **Naval Museum**.

Behind the harbour and the fortifications is the heart of the **old town**, an atmospheric maze of little alleyways and streets with some wonderful examples of antique Turkish balconies and Venetian façades. It has become one of the trendiest areas in the city for **craft shops**, particularly in and around Theotokopoúlou Street (named after El Greco). Near here you'll come across the elegant **Renieri Gate**, with an inscription from 1608.

### Archaeological Museum ✴✴✴

The inconspicuous exterior of the museum (open 08:00–19:00/20:00 Tues–Fri, and until 14:30 Sat–Sun, closed Monday, tel: 0821-90334/20334) gives no hint of its elegant interior: once the Venetian church of San Francesco, the vaulted space inside is the perfect setting for this well laid-out collection. As well as Minoan pottery, there are some interesting *pithoi* (storage jars) and *larnakes* – decorated stone sarcophagi – one of which still

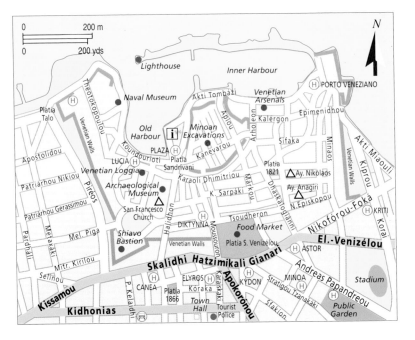

holds skeletal remains. Graeco-Roman sculptures, glassware and some vibrant mosaics are grouped towards the rear of the museum, whilst in the tranquil little courtyard you can seen an old Turkish **fountain-house** and the remains of a **minaret** which date from the time when the church was converted into a mosque by the Turks.

## Cretan Museum **
Hidden away in the cloisters of the Catholic church, the Cretan Museum (open 09:00–13:00 and 18:00–21:00 Mon to Fri, 09:00–14:00 Sat, closed Sun and holidays, tel: 0821-23273) houses old looms, tapestries and interesting folkloric set-pieces.

## Naval Museum
Modern models of ships and submarines mingle with historical relics and scenarios from great sea battles (open 10:00–14:00 Tues–Sun, tel: 0821-91875/55301).

## Historical Museum and Archives *
A rather dusty collection of oddments, ranging from old photographs to exhibits focusing on the Cretan struggle for independence. The museum (open 08:00–13:00, Mon to Fri, tel: 0821-42606) also houses an extensive archive collection.

**A MAJOR PILGRIMAGE**

St John the Hermit, who was influential in re-establishing Christianity on Crete during the early 11th century, lived in a remote cave on Akrotíri for the latter part of his life. It's said that he met his end when he was shot by a hunter who mistook him for a wild animal. On St John's feast day, 7 October, a huge pilgrimage is made to Akrotíri. The supplicants go first to the Monastery of Gouvernétou, where they are blessed by the bishop. The long trek down to the cave itself is then made by all those who are fit enough.

## Akrotíri Peninsula **

Jutting out to the east of Haniá, the Akrotíri Peninsula separates the Bay of Haniá from the huge, sheltered anchorage of the Bay of Sóudha on the other side of the isthmus. A tour around the peninsula makes for an enjoyable half or full day excursion from the city.

The **Bay of Sóudha** itself is an important naval anchorage (no photographs permitted) and the docking point for Piraeus ferries. Behind the bay is a large NATO installation (which allegedly houses cruise missiles targeted at Libya) and the airport, but once you have got past these the real interest begins as the lowland part of the peninsula gives way to the steep hills and cliffs at the tip of Akrotíri.

The first stop is at the large and well-preserved **Monastery of Ayía Triádha** (open 07:00–14:00 and 17:00–19:00 daily), built in the Venetian Renaissance style in the 17th century. The grandiose entrance façade leads through to a central courtyard dominated by the monastery **church**, which has an elaborate *iconostasis* (altar wall) and a collection of interesting frescoes – some of which are modern. You can climb up beside the **bell**

*The monastery of Ayía Triádha was built by a family of Venetian merchants, the Tzangaroli, and has always been a wealthy foundation thanks to its extensive landholdings planted with olives and vineyards, which are still tended by the monks.*

**tower** for a panorama of the surrounding plains and the extensive olive groves owned by the monastery. Inside the entrance a small **museum** houses icons of the 16th and 17th centuries as well as some intriguing wood-cut amulets and a parchment scroll dating from the 12th century.

Continue past Ayía Triádha for another 4km (2.5 miles) and, after passing through a scenic little gorge, you'll arrive at the **Monastery of Gouvernétou** (open 07:00–12:00 and 15:00–19:00 daily). This lonely, isolated monastery is surrounded by nothing but rock, with the cliffs plunging down towards the sea just a few metres away. The atmosphere of the setting is heightened by its contrast with the tranquil, tree-filled courtyard inside the monastery's daunting walls. Take a close look at the façade of the **monastery church**, where monsters' heads and other embellishments are strangely out of keeping with the Venetian style. There's also a small **museum** with a collection of icons.

The more adventurous can set off from here for a walk (a round trip of around two hours) to the ruins of the **Monastery of Katholikó**, set dramatically at the base of a ravine. This monastery was abandoned in the 16th century because of the constant threat of pirate attacks. Just before it is the **Cave of St John**, a deep, dark cavern with numerous stalactites dripping down from the roof.

Backtracking past Ayía Triádha and heading toward the western side of the peninsula brings you to the beach at **Stavrós** where, after your morning tour, you can relax and order lunch in one of the beach-side tavernas. A superb little beach with safe swimming, Stavrós is backed by massive cliffs; its main claim to fame is that it was used as the setting for the climactic final scenes of the film *Zorba The Greek*. It's also the most popular beach for day-trips from Haniá, and can become very crowded in high season.

Heading back towards the city you pass the **tomb of Venizélos**, where Eleftheríos Venizélos and his son Sophocles are buried. It's a fitting setting, overlooking the former capital to the west.

*Curious sculptures adorn the façade of the Monastery of Gouvernétou on the Akrotíri peninsula.*

## Georgioúpolis **

Set at the base of Cape Dhrápano, this charming village
has received considerable coverage as one of the best
resorts in Crete but it still manages to retain a peaceful,
low-key atmosphere.

Part of Georgioúpolis' appeal lies in the fact that it
always seems green and fresh: the **Almirós River** flows
past on the north side of the village, providing irrigation
for the thickets of eucalyptus and cypress trees which
surround the village.

Groves of bamboo provide some protection to the
beach, which shelves gently into the sea and runs for
miles to the east of Georgioúpolis. The area immediately
next to the village has safe bathing, but beware of offshore currents on the more exposed stretches. There's a
second sandy beach on the other side of the river estuary.

In the centre of the village is a large square, shaded
by massive old eucalyptus trees, where you can sit and
watch the world go by. There are several good tavernas
around the square, specializing in seafood.

*A peaceful quayside scene
in the delightful village of
Georgioúpolis, where daily
life proceeds at a leisurely
pace in spite of its attractions as a holiday resort.*

## Lake Kournás *

A popular walk from Georgioúpolis is to scenic Lake
Kournás, 4km (2.5 miles) inland. Crete's only natural
freshwater lake, Kournás is the picture of tranquillity,
with its deep blue waters reflecting the surrounding hills
and mountain slopes. You can, of course, also drive up to
the lake, which is a favourite spot for locals' barbecues at
weekends. There's one small taverna, with canoes and
pedalos for rent, on the lakeshore. Like the nearby
Almirós River, Lake Kournás is a good place for bird-
watching: there's a footpath around the shore, and the
circuit takes around an hour.

## Rodhópou Peninsula *

Extending 18km (11 miles) out from the northern coastline, Rodhópou is a lonely, rugged peninsula with very
few decent roads but several adventurous hiking trails.

At the base of the peninsula, **Kolimbári** is an attractive little village with a long pebble beach and several

*The only freshwater lake on the island, Lake Kournás mirrors the surrounding hills in its crystalline waters.*

fish tavernas – it's a popular spot for an evening out from Haniá in the summer months. Just past the village on the east side of the peninsula is the **Moní Gonía**, which was founded in the 17th century and contains an important collection of icons. The monastery (open daily, closed 14:00–17:00) has suffered numerous attacks (mostly from the Turks, whose cannonballs can still be seen lodged in the wall facing the sea) and at one point its magnificent library was burned down, but it has been rebuilt time and time again. The main icon collection is housed in a small museum within the quadrangle, with those by the Cretan painter Konstantinos Palaiokapas amongst the most precious. North of the monastery is the modern Orthodox Academy of Crete.

The road continues for just over 3km (2 miles) to the tiny village of **Afráta**, surrounded by vineyards and olive groves. From here you can double back down a dirt track to reach the peninsula's main village, **Rodhópou**, which has several cafés and tavernas for refreshments.

Beyond here, you'll need to be well-equipped for hiking in order to reach the ancient sanctuary of **Diktynna** at the tip of the peninsula, or the small chapel of **Áyios Ioánnis** on the west coast. The Diktynna was the most important sanctuary in western Crete during Roman times, and several statues from the temple are now in the Haniá Museum. The arduous trek to the chapel of Áyios Ioánnis is made by thousands of people on 29 August each year in honour of St John the Baptist, culminating in the mass baptism of boys called John.

**BY BOAT TO THE SANCTUARY**

The sanctuary of Diktynna on the Rodhópou Peninsula was dedicated to the goddess of the same name, who was especially venerated in this part of the island. A nature goddess and huntress, her sanctuary was said to have been guarded by massive hounds which the Cretans claim were as strong as bears. A good way to visit the temple is on a boat trip from Haniá; the boats head here for the sheltered swimming in the cove beneath the temple, and there's plenty of time to explore the ruins as well. Contact the EOT in Haniá for details of day trips.

## ISLAND UPS AND DOWNS

The fact that the whole of ancient Falásarna is now high and dry some 100m (330ft) inland is proof that around 25,000 years ago the whole of Crete's western coastline rose between 6–9m (20–30ft) due to the shifting of tectonic plates beneath the Aegean. As this end of the island was forced up out of the water, sections of eastern Crete were submerged – causing, for instance, the **Sunken City** at Eloúndha (see page 68).

*The wide sweep of Falásarna Bay, one of the best beaches on the west coast, is protected by the headland of Cape Koutrí to the north.*

## Falásarna and the Wild West Coast ★★★

Beyond the Rodhópou Peninsula the coastal road continues to **Kastélli Kissámou**, a pleasant town with no tourist attractions to speak of but plenty of genuine, local *kafenía* around the main square as well as shops and other services such as banks.

The new road continues to the village of **Plátanos**, where there is a junction with signposts to **Falásarna**. This is a detour well worth making, even though the wonderful **beach** at Falásarna is no longer the well-kept secret it once was. As you descend a series of hairpin bends down the hillside, a huge bay opens out before you with the broad, sandy crescent of the beach sweeping round to the headland of Cape Koutrí beyond.

Much of the broad plain behind the beach has been taken over by the ubiquitous plastic polytunnels for growing salad crops; at the end of the tarmac road there are a couple of tavernas, a beach bar and a campsite. The beach itself shelves gently into the azure waters, with plenty of room for everyone to spread themselves out.

When you've had enough sun and sand you can amble along a rough track to the site of **ancient Falásarna**, around 2km (1 mile) to the north. Amongst the ruins of house walls and a round tower are a series of canals leading to the sea; just behind the site there's a

large, rock-cut 'throne' sitting in the middle of the undergrowth – its origins and purpose are still the subject of speculation.

## Elafonísi ★★★

The second major beach on the wild west coast is Elafonísi, at the opposite extremity in the far south. There are two ways to get there: you can drive on from

*Perched in isolation on a rocky promontory, the monastery of Hrysoskalítissa was founded here in the 13th century, though the present church is much more recent. Now a nunnery, its name derives from the legend of its golden step, 'hrissí skála'.*

Plátanos around the spectacular **coast road**, which is mostly unpaved but easily negotiable – and new asphalt sections are being laid continuously. Winding around the cliffs, with dizzying drops to the Aegean below, the road passes above the Bay of Sfinári and the Bay of Stomióu before arriving at the **Monastery of Hrysoskalítissa** on the southern headland. This is also where the **inland road** from Kastélli Kissámou emerges, having traversed the ridges and ravines of the mountains in between.

A further 5km (3 miles) brings you to the extraordinary **beach** at Elafonísi: what makes it stand out from anywhere else in Crete is that it seems virtually tropical, with the pale pink and white sand dipping very gently into a shallow lagoon of warm, aquamarine water. Elafonísi is in fact the small **island** just offshore, which you can wade across to in knee-deep water.

There's plenty of shade under the trees behind the beach, and a couple of snack bars open in season. As yet, development hasn't reached Elafonísi but there are rumoured to be plans in the pipeline. Meanwhile, it remains an idyllic spot despite its popularity. You can also reach Elafonísi on a daily bus from Haniá, or twice-daily boats from Paleóhora.

### THE GOLDEN STEP

The 13th-century Monastery of Hrysoskalitissa is dedicated to Our Lady of the Golden Stair; there are 90 steps leading down to the sea from the pinnacle on which it is built, and one of these is said to be made of pure gold – but it is only visible to those who are without sin. Let us know if you can see it!

### CHESTNUT FESTIVAL

On the inland route towards Elafonísi you'll pass through some lovely chestnut plantations: although not as extensive as they used to be, they still form the basis of the local economy in the attractive, tree-lined village of **Élos**. A major chestnut festival takes place here in late October – check with the EOT in Haniá for exact dates.

**WINDSURFERS' PARADISE**

For high intermediate and advanced board sailors, Paleóhora has some of the most reliable **wind patterns** in Crete – if not in Greece. On average, five afternoons a week will have winds of Force 4 or greater for most of the summer. These favourable conditions drew three English instructors to set up their own school here, and **Westwind** now has a comprehensive range of over 40 boards and 50 slalom and wave rigs for hire. There are also German and Greek windsurf schools on the beach. Packages with Westwind, including instruction (if required) and unlimited windsurfing are available for six-day periods throughout the summer. This is a very popular centre, and pre-booking is recommended.

## Paleóhora **

Built on a small peninsula jutting out into the sea, the village of Paleóhora is almost completely surrounded by water. With the rugged south face of the Lefká Óri sloping down to the coast behind it, the village is in an undeniably attractive position and has developed rapidly in recent years to become the busiest resort at the west end of this coastline.

So far, Paleóhora has been spared concrete-block hotels: on the west side of the bay, you'll see a massive building site with its own road system under construction – this is not, as might be thought, the beginnings of mass tourism, but in fact an entirely new village being built by the locals who've grown rich on tourism and decided to move away from the noise of all the thriving bars and discos in the old village!

On the west side of the village there's a superb sandy **beach**, spacious enough never to seem crowded, with tamarisk trees for shade. This is a prime **windsurfing** venue. One of the great advantages of Paleóhora is that if it's too windy on this beach for sunbathing, you can go through the village to another sheltered (although pebbly) beach on the east side.

Paleóhora's mulberry-lined main street, Venizélou, is closed to traffic every evening as the restaurant and café owners spread their tables and chairs outside to create a chaotic, lively promenade where tourists and locals eat, drink and carouse from table to table. At the end of the main street is a small headland with a ruined fort, with the old harbour on one side of it and a new marina on the other side.

Despite the ever-increasing numbers of people who have discovered Paleóhora's charms it remains very relaxed and low-key, and is an excellent base for exploring this part of Crete: there are daily boats to **Elafonísi**, twice-weekly trips to **Gávdos**, plenty of good walks along the coast to the east or back into the mountains, and it's also a good location from which to walk the **Samariá Gorge**, with direct boats back from Ayía Rouméli.

## Azoyirés *

A worthwhile excursion from Paleóhora is to the mountain village of Azoyirés, 8km (5 miles) to the northeast. Surrounded by pines, cypresses, olive and maple trees, this peaceful village has a tiny **museum** (open 09:00–14:00 weekends only) with some intriguing material from the Turkish occupation. Just outside the village is a series of **caves** in which lived several dozen monks during the 11th century. Steps in the cave lead down to a small shrine dedicated to these early missionaries.

*Elafonísi, where the sea shells on the beach give a pink tinge to the fine white sand.*

## Samariá Gorge ***

Considered one of the 'unmissable' experiences of Crete, the hike down through the Samariá Gorge is the second most popular excursion on the island for visitors (Knossós being the first) with as many as 400,000 people making the 16km (10 mile) trip during each summer. Impressive though the gorge is, don't expect to be able to appreciate it in solitude: communing with nature isn't on the agenda when two or three thousand other hikers are treading on your heels.

Despite the vast numbers who do actually make it through the gorge, the walk should not be underestimated. It involves five or six hours of fairly strenuous hiking over rough ground, so you should be reasonably fit, accustomed to walks of this length, and be properly equipped with sturdy shoes or boots. Heart attacks, broken legs and even fatalities are not unknown here. The

---

**THE RUINED FORT**

On the tiny headland at Paleóhora are the remains of an ancient fort, built by the Venetians in 1279. Known as the **Kastél Selínou**, or the Castle of Selinos, it stood for around 250 years before being pillaged by the pirate Barbarossa in the mid-16th century. It was never rebuilt.

trip is only possible between May and October, since during the winter months the stream which runs through the gorge is often swollen to flood proportions, and certain sections are impassable.

Most people walk the gorge as part of a day excursion, taking a coach to the starting point, walking down, taking a boat from Ayía Rouméli at the bottom of the gorge to Hóra Sfakíon, then a coach back home again. Boats also depart from Ayía Rouméli to Paleóhora, Soúyia and Loutró.

Although coaches pick up from all over the island, it means an early start and a long journey home at the end of the day if you're staying in, say, eastern Crete. It's an easy option if you're based in Haniá or nearby, and you'll also be at an advantage staying in one of the resorts on the south coast, since you can start walking before it gets too hot and then there's just a boat ride back at the end.

The gorge begins on the edge of the **Plain of Omalós**, in the heart of the Lefká Óri. Here, there is a large coach and car park, refreshment stalls, and a warden's office. The **descent** starts on the **xylóskalon** (wooden stairway), a stepped path cut out from the rock which zigzags down between huge old cypresses, with the looming limestone massif of Mount Gíngilos rising up on the right-hand side. At this stage, the track drops around 800m (2600ft) within the first 2km (1 mile). Near the bottom is the little chapel of **Áyios Nikólaos**, where there are benches to rest on. The route levels out from here on, crisscrossing the cool, clear waters of the stream. The gorge is fairly wide at this point, and it's a good place to look for rare plants and flowers.

Around the halfway mark, about 7km (4 miles) from the start of the gorge,

*The dramatic view at the start of the strenuous and exciting walk down the Samariá Gorge.*

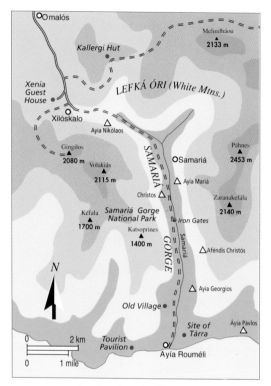

Chionodoxa cretica, *the delicate Cretan Glory of the Snow, growing in the mountains at the top of the Samariá Gorge. Rare flowering plants are one of the features of the gorge.*

you come to the abandoned village of **Samariá**. The inhabitants of this ancient settlement were relocated when the park was created in 1962.

Shortly after the village there is a small whitewashed chapel on the right-hand side, signalling the beginning of the most dramatic section of the track. The walls of the gorge gradually begin to narrow down, and the path cuts across from one side of the stream to the other until you arrive at the Iron Gates, or **Sidherespórtes**. This is the narrowest part of the gorge, with the two rock walls rising up 300m (1000ft) almost next to each other, framing the blue sky above. There are just a few metres between each side at the bottom, with the stream entirely filling the gap; you have to proceed along a plank walk to cross the Iron Gates.

> **THE EASY WAY**
>
> Many tour operators advertize Samariá 'the easy way', which involves catching the boat from Hóra Sfakíon to Ayía Rouméli and then walking up to the Sidherespórtes and back down again. This should take 2 hours at most, and is an appealing option if you don't feel fit enough to tackle the whole thing. You miss out on some of the most attractive parts of the gorge, but will at least get to see the dramatic Iron Gates.

*The towering, evocatively named Sidherespórtes, or Iron Gates, at the bottom of the Samariá Gorge. The narrow gap between the two spectacular vertical rock walls is filled by the stream flowing down the gorge, and walkers negotiate it along a plank walk.*

## THE ÍMBROS RAVINE

If you're a keen walker and the thought of the crowds in the Samariá Gorge puts you off, you could hike instead down the Ímbros Ravine which opens out onto the coast to the east of Hóra Sfakíon. Although on a smaller scale than Samariá, it shares similar features and the path is an easy, 3 hour walk alongside the stream that runs through the ravine. The track starts just south of the village of Ímbros, on the Askifou Plateau.

Once through the Iron Gates the gorge opens out into a broader valley, with the ruined village of **old Ayía Rouméli** and the park hut where you must hand in your ticket. From here, it's a further twenty minutes walk to the sea and modern **Ayía Rouméli**. Most people head straight for the beach, where a plunge into the waves soothes aching muscles and feet. There are also plenty of tavernas and bars on hand to slake your thirst and assuage your appetite, and even a hotel or two – although few people would wish to stay here, since the village is completely characterless and solely geared to earning its income for just a few hours every afternoon when the walkers arrive. If you're really stuck for something to do, you can climb the headland to the ruins of a Turkish fort, just above the walkway to the gorge. From the quay, ferries depart for Paleóhora, Loutró and Hóra Sfakíon.

## Loutró ★★★

The ultimate in 'hideaway' resorts, Loutró is a gem of a village tucked away beneath the rocky headlands of the south coast. It can only be reached by boat from Hóra Sfakíon (or a longish walk along the coastal path), so there are no roads, no cars – just the tranquillity of a perfect little bay, with the water sparkling blue beyond the shingle beach. The only event which disturbs the peace here is the arrival of the ferries which put in regularly as they ply the coastline.

Don't expect late-night raves – Loutró closes down early, with just the lapping of the waves not far from your window to lull you to sleep after an evening at one of the few simple but excellent tavernas along the shore. The whole place is kept neat and tidy, with nearly all the houses decked out in blue and white paint.

Swimmers and snorkellers will find many little rocky coves nearby to explore, reached by footpath or canoes (which can be hired in the village). Nearby, **Sweetwater Beach** is a large, sandy semicircle beneath towering cliffs where several bubbling springs emerge from the sands; there's a daily boat from Loutró, and there are also boats to **Mármara Beach**, another pretty cove with rock caves behind it.

*The Askífou Plateau at the heart of the White Mountains. The ruins of a Turkish castle crown the conical hill, in a commanding position overlooking the plain.*

*The ancient fort of Frangokástello, said to be haunted by the ghosts of a phantom army. Only the outer walls of this Venetian stronghold survive.*

### Hóra Sfakíon

The 'capital' of the Sfakiá region, this tiny port wedged between the mountains and the sea is nowadays little more than a transit point for weary walkers ferried back from Ayía Rouméli, who rejoin their coaches here. It has all the usual shops, tavernas and hotels, but there is little point in lingering.

A plaque on the seafront marks the spot where some 10,000 Allied soldiers were evacuated after the Battle of Crete. There were once over 100 churches in Hóra Sfakíon, but most were destroyed during the war.

### Frangokástello **

Dominated by the shell of an old Venetian **castle**, Frangokástello is set on a marshy bay with a small fishing harbour and a wonderful, sandy **beach** stretching around to a lighthouse at the western end. The beach is very popular with campers and backpackers (although sometimes sandflies can be a nuisance here), and there are rooms for rent and tavernas in the village. Another large, deserted beach lies just to the west of this bay.

The rectangular **castle** looks solid enough from afar,

---

**THE HAUNTED CASTLE**

In 1828, during the War of Independence against the Turks, an adventurer named Hatzimichális Daliánnis made a heroic last stand in the castle of Frangokástello against the advancing Turks. Locals warned him to take to the hills, but instead he and his 385 men were massacred here by the superior Turkish forces. They lie buried in the coastal sands, and it's said that each year on 17 May, the anniversary of the battle, this phantom army rises up to parade past the fort. They are known as the *drossoulítes* or 'spirits of the dew', since they always appear in the dawn mists.

but once you approach it becomes clear that only a shell remains, with a tower at each corner; the largest tower, on the southwest corner, acted as a guardhouse for the main gateway (the Venetian Lion of St Mark can still be seen above the gate). Built in 1371, the fort was the scene of a tragic incident in the 19th century which locals claim has left it haunted.

## Gávdos Island *

This isolated island is the biggest and most southerly of those lying off Crete. Inhabited by no more than 50 people it seems at first to be nothing but barren rock, but inland pines and other plants (including wild thyme, from which the local bees make good honey) add a touch of greenery. Goats amble across the scrubland, and in spring and autumn migratory birds rest here on their long journey across the Libyan Sea.

With 50km (31 miles) of sea separating it from the mainland, Gávdos is not the easiest of places to reach. During the summer boats cross regularly from Paleóhora and Hóra Sfakíon, but during the winter there is only the occasional supply boat. You can camp or rent rooms on the island, but water (and sometimes food) is in short supply.

The main attraction of Gávdos is its sheer isolation, and you could hike around much of its low-lying terrain without seeing another soul. The boats dock at the tiny harbour of **Karabé**, from where it's a one-hour walk (or a slow ride in one of the tractor-trailers which meet the boats) up to the island capital of **Kastrí**. There's a shop (which also serves as post and telephone office) and a school (with one teacher and one pupil!) and that's about it. Most people head from here to the long, sandy beach of **Sarakiníko** on the northeast coast, where there are several basic tavernas and a fair number of hippie residents. The other main beach is **Koúrfos**, to the south, which has a taverna and a couple of rooms to rent. There's also a small beach next to the promontory of **Tripití**, which lays claim to being the very southernmost point in the whole of Europe.

---

**A DWINDLING COMMUNITY**

Occupied since Neolithic times, Gávdos was known to the Romans (who called it Clauda) and St Paul was driven past here during a storm on his voyage to Rome – which ended instead in a shipwreck on Malta. In the Middle Ages it supported some 8000 inhabitants, herding sheep and goats on what was then a fertile island. By the beginning of this century the population had shrunk to 1400 people, but the island's resources have gradually been exhausted and those few families who now remain scrape a meagre living from the barren soil.

# Western Crete at a Glance

Olympic Airways has four flights daily (flight time 45 minutes) from **Athens** airport (West terminal), and flights from Hania to **Thessaloniki** twice weekly. Air Greece also flies Athens-Haniá. There are also **charters** direct to Haniá from the UK and other European departure points. The **airport** is on the Akrotíri Peninsula, 15km (9 miles) from the town centre: Olympic flights are met by a bus, otherwise taxis are available.

**Ferries** from Piraeus take around 12 hours on an overnight sailing, with daily departures. They dock in the port of **Soúdha**, 10km (6 miles) from Haniá, from where there are buses and taxis to the city.

Frequent **bus** connections link Haniá with Iraklion, Réthimnon and towns and villages throughout western Crete. The bus station is on Odhós Kidhonías, close to the city centre.

Haniá itself is compact enough for everything to be within walking distance. For exploring further afield, **cars** can be rented from **Hertz**, **Avis** or local outfits such as **Speed Rent-a-Car**, 105 Hálidon, tel (0821) 44768 and **Tellus Travel**, 1 Smirnis, tel (0821) 50400, fax 91716.

A good place for hiring **bikes** is **Zeus**, 38 Karaolí, tel (0821) 57457.

*Haniá*
**Amphora**, 20 Parodos Theotokopóulou St, Haniá 73100, tel/fax (0821) 93224. On the harbour front (and can therefore be noisy), superbly renovated 14th-century building with charming rooms. (A)
**Creta Paradise Beach Resort**, Gerani, Haniá 73100, tel (0821) 61315, fax (0821) 61134. On the beach in Gerani, 12km (8 miles) west of Haniá, this comfortable resort with full amenities (including pool, watersports, tennis etc) makes a good base if you don't want to be in the city. (A)
**Casa Delfino**, 9 Theofánous St, Haniá 73100, tel (0821) 93098, fax (0821) 96500. In the heart of the old town, this sumptuous 17th-century Venetian mansion has 12 luxurious apartments. (B)
**Doma**, 124 Venizélou, Haniá 73100, tel (0821) 51772, fax (0821) 41578. Another fascinating hotel, in an elegantly furnished neoclassical mansion just along the seafront from the city centre. (B)
**Rodon**, 92 Akrotírious St, Haniá 73100, tel (0821) 58317, fax (0821) 56821. Interesting, modern hotel on the east side of the city with views over the bay. (B)
**El Greco**, 49 Theotokopóulou St, Haniá 73100, tel (0821) 90432, fax (0821) 91829. Quiet little family-run hotel, with roof garden, in the old quarter. (B)

**Pension Eva**, 1 Theofánous and Zambelíou St, Haniá 73100, tel (0821) 76706. Immaculate, period-style rooms with *en suite* facilities. Roof terrace. (B)
**Pension Nostos**, 42-6 Zambelíou, Haniá 73100, tel (0821) 94740, fax (0821) 54502. Another superb little pension in the back streets: 12 studios (some with sea views). (B)
*Georgioúpolis*
**Georgioúpolis Beach Hotel**, Georgioúpolis 73007, tel (0825) 61012, fax (0825) 61034. New complex between the town and the beach; pool. (B)
**Tarra Apartments**, Georgioúpolis 73007, tel (0825) 61324. Attractive apartments with kitchenettes and balconies, surrounded by luxuriant gardens. (C)
**Nostalgie Apartments**, Georgioúpolis 73007, tel (0825) 61327. Well-kept apartments (with spacious verandahs). (C)
*Paleóhora*
**Pal Beach Hotel**, Paleóhora 73001, tel (0823) 41512. Conveniently situated, many rooms with balconies overlooking the west beach. (B)
**Hotel Elman**, Paleóhora 73001, tel (0823) 41414, fax (0823) 41412. A modern block, but handy for the windsurfing school on its doorstep. (B)
**Toni Mari Apartments**, Paleóhora 73001, tel (0823) 41787. Family-run studios/

apartments surrounding a flower-filled courtyard just across from the beach. (C)
**Kastello**, Paleóhora 73001, tel (0821) 41143. Nestling under the fort at the end of the bay, this clean, friendly hotel has lovely views. (C)

*Loutró*
**Porto Loutró**, Hóra Sfakíon, tel (0825) 91227. Superb little hotel with charming rooms. (B)
**The Blue House**, Hóra Sfakíon, tel (0825) 91127. Friendly pension in a traditional house; all rooms have balconies overlooking the bay. (B)

## WHERE TO EAT

*Haniá*
**Taman**, 49 Zambelíou. Very popular restaurant in the basement of old Turkish baths, vegetarian and unusual Greek dishes. Young, lively atmosphere but can be hot and stuffy.
**The Well of the Turk**, 1-3 Kalinikou Sarpaki, Splazia, tel (0821) 54547. This restaurant serves a unique blend of Greek and Turkish cuisine.
**Akrolimano**, Neo Hora, tel (0821) 94230. Excellent fish specialities. Popular with locals so can get busy.
**Karnáyio**, Platia Katehaki, tel (0821) 53366. Close to the Venetian arsenals, set back in a quiet square overlooking moored yachts, this has a wide menu of traditional Cretan food.
**Konaki**, 40 Kondiláki, tel (0821) 70859. In the heart of the old town, Cretan speciali-

ties and live music in a flower-filled courtyard.
**Dino's**, Inner Harbour, tel (0821) 57448. Receives consistently good reviews for its reasonably priced seafood.
**Ovras**, 24 Skoufon, tel (0821) 87170. Spilling out into a narrow alleyway, with musicians wandering between the tables. Greek specialities.
**Ekstra**, 8 Zambelíou, tel (0821) 75725. Friendly little restaurant behind the old harbour, reasonably priced.

*Georgioúpolis*
**To Arkadi**. Consistently good food at this attractive taverna by the river mouth.
**Café Georgioúpolis Pub**. This is one of the most popular of the many busy places on the main square.

*Paleóhora*
**Corelli**. An excellent little restaurant on the eastern side of town; Greek food.
**Nike**. Terrific pizzas cooked in a wood-fired oven. On the beach road.
**Jetée**. An excellent place for an evening cocktail, watching the sun go down to the west.
**Caravella**, tel (0823) 41131. Overlooking the sweep of the bay this friendly family-run taverna serves fish specialities and good home cuisine.

**Dionisos**. One of the best of the traditional tavernas, where you can choose from the kitchen. Good value.

*Loutró*
**The Blue House**, tel (0825) 91127. Outstanding seafood, vegetarian and Greek dishes served on the quayside.

## TOURS AND EXCURSIONS

All the standard island excursions (**Knossós**, the **Samariá Gorge** and so on) are available from travel agents in Haniá. **Creta Wave**, tel (0821) 81549, operate daily trips along the coast to the **Bay of Almirída** and then on for lunch at **Maráthi**. Rock climbing, trekking, mountain bike tours and even skiing can be organized through **Trekking Plan** (Mountain Climbing Bureau), Karaoli Dimitriou 15, tel (0825) 44946.

## USEFUL CONTACTS

**Tourist Office**, 1st Floor, 40 Kriari St, Haniá, tel (0821) 92943. Open: Mon–Fri 08:00–19:00, Sat 09:00–14:00.
**Police**, tel (0821) 51111.
**Olympic Airways** 88, Tzanakaki, Haniá, tel (0821) 40268.

| PALEÓHORA | J | F | M | A | M | J | J | A | S | O | N | D |
|---|---|---|---|---|---|---|---|---|---|---|---|---|
| AVERAGE TEMP. °F | 59 | 59 | 63 | 68 | 75 | 84 | 88 | 88 | 84 | 77 | 68 | 63 |
| AVERAGE TEMP. °C | 15 | 15 | 17 | 20 | 24 | 29 | 31 | 31 | 29 | 25 | 20 | 17 |
| Hours of Sun Daily | 5 | 5 | 6 | 8 | 10 | 12 | 13 | 12 | 9 | 6 | 5 | 5 |
| RAINFALL " | 3 | 2 | 2 | 0.5 | 0 | 0 | 0 | 0 | 0 | 0.5 | 2 | 2 |
| RAINFALL mm | 88 | 48 | 39 | 15 | 2 | 3 | 0 | 0 | 1 | 12 | 43 | 47 |
| Days of Rainfall | 9 | 8 | 6 | 3 | 1 | 0 | 0 | 0 | 1 | 3 | 6 | 9 |

| CONVERSION CHART | | |
|---|---|---|
| **FROM** | **TO** | **MULTIPLY BY** |
| Millimetres | inches | 0.0394 |
| Metres | yards | 1.0936 |
| Metres | feet | 3.281 |
| Kilometres | miles | 0.6214 |
| Hectares | acres | 2.471 |
| Litres | pints | 1.760 |
| Kilograms | pounds | 2.205 |
| Tonnes | tons | 0.984 |

To convert Celsius to Fahrenheit: x 9 ÷ 5 + 32

There are no limits on the amount of travellers cheques and foreign currency imported, although you should declare currency amounts over US$1000 if you expect to take it out again.

**Currency exchange**: Banks and post offices offer better exchange rates than hotel bureaux, although you may find there are long queues in the banks. Always take your passport with you when cashing travellers cheques or changing currency. Some travel agents and tourist offices will also change travellers cheques, and there are also dedicated bureaux de change in some resort areas.

**Credit cards**: Major credit cards are widely accepted in hotels, restaurants, petrol stations and resort shops, but don't expect to be able to use them in small, out-of-the-way tavernas or remote villages. Cash advances on credit cards are available at the major bank branches; holders of Visa and American Express cards can make 24-hour cash withdrawals from ATM machines at branches of the Credit Bank in Réthimnon,

Haniá, Hersónissos and Iráklion. These machines also exchange foreign banknotes.

**Tipping**: Tipping is normal in Crete, even though the amounts given are often fairly small. Service charges of 10 to 15% are usually included in restaurant and hotel bills, and you should tip the waiter your small change on top of this if service has been good. Hotel porters, maids and taxi drivers will also usually expect a tip.

## Accommodation

There is a vast range of accommodation on offer in Crete, ranging from simple, white-washed rooms in village houses to luxurious bungalows in beach hotel complexes.

All **hotels** are classified into six grades. A list including most hotels on the island is available from the **EOT**. The categories start with deluxe ('L') and run down from A to E. Prices in each category are controlled by the government, and they must be displayed on the back of the room door.

In the high season many of the luxury hotels and those in the top categories are fully booked by overseas tour oper-

ators, but if you're stuck you can be sure that a room will be found for you somewhere. Outside July and August much more is available and there are also plenty of decent, clean B or C class hotels, at which renting out rooms for the night is more acceptable than it is in the package hotels. D and E class hotels tend to be very basic indeed, although reasonable prices compensate for the lack of amenities.

**Self-catering villas** are an attractive option and there are many superb properties for rent. However, the majority of these are contracted to specialist self-catering operators and you're unlikely to find a good one by just turning up on the island.

Independent travellers and backpackers tend to stay in **private rooms**, which are also controlled and graded from A to C. Most of these were once in family homes, offering an opportunity really to get to know the Cretans and experience their legendary hospitality. Nowadays many of these rooms are in characterless, purpose-built blocks but away from the main resort areas you can still find simple, pleasant rooms which cost next to nothing. Signs usually indicate 'Rent Rooms' or 'Zimmer Frei'.

## Business Hours

The Cretans start the day early, between 07:00–08:00; a long morning's work is followed by lunch, and then there is the all-important siesta, which lasts from

## GOOD READING

Cadogan, Gerald (1980) *Palaces of Minoan Crete*. Routledge. Davaras, Costis *Guide to Cretan Antiquities*. Noyes Press; Eptalofolos, Athens. Godfrey, Jonnie and Karslake, Elizabeth

(1986, 1987) *Landscapes of Eastern Crete* and *Landscapes of Western Crete*. Sunflower Press. Excellent pocket guides, essential for country rambles. Huxley, Anthony and Taylor, William (1989)

*Flowers of Greece and the Aegean*. Hogarth Press. Kazantzakis, Nikos (1959) *Zorba the Greek*. Faber. Moss, W. Stanley (1971) *Ill Met by Moonlight*. Buchan & Enright. Recounts the

kidnapping of General Kreipe. Psychoundákis, George (1955) *The Cretan Runner*. John Murray; Transatlantic Arts. The author was a courier for the resistance: a lively read.

around 14:00–16:00. By late afternoon, shops and offices start to open up again and generally stay open fairly late – often until 21:00.

**Shops**: Usually open from around 08:00–15:00, closing for the rest of the afternoon on Mon, Wed and Sat. Other afternoons they're open from 17:30–20:30, although there are many local variations. Most are closed on Sun. Souvenir shops and other tourist-oriented businesses often open all day, 7 days a week.

**Banks**: 08:00–14:00 Mon to Thur, 08:00–15:30 Fri; some branches in tourist areas open again in the evenings and on Sat mornings for exchange facilities.

**Post offices**: Open 08:00–14:00 in most places, 08:00–19:00 (sometimes 20:00) in the main towns.

## Time

Greek time is 2 hours ahead of Greenwich Mean Time, 1 hour ahead of Central European Time, 7 hours ahead of US Eastern Standard Winter Time. Clocks go forward 1 hour on last Sun in Mar, back on last Sun in Sep.

## Communications

**Post**: Post offices deal with all the usual services as well as some additional ones such as currency exchange, but telephones are dealt with separately. As well as the regular post offices (identifiable by a yellow sign) there are also mobile post offices, open longer hours, which are set up in resort areas over the summer. Stamps can also be bought at street kiosks, although they attract a small mark-up. The poste restante service is widely used and efficient.

**Telephone**: Most towns have an office of OTE, the Greek telecommunications organization, where you make calls from a cubicle and pay afterwards. Local calls can be made from metered telephone kiosks – often located in the *kafenion* in small places. Telephone card kiosks are also widespread.

## Electricity

220 volts AC.

## Weights and Measures

Greece uses the metric system.

## Health Precautions

**Water** on Crete is safe to drink, and indeed you should consume plenty of liquid in the summer months to compensate for the loss of body fluids due to the heat.

**Sunstroke** can be a problem if you expose yourself too quickly to begin with, and sunburn can occur even on hazy days. Wear a hat or otherwise cover up during the hottest period of the day, and work on your tan gradually.

**Mosquitoes** are easily dealt with by burning pyrethrum insect coils or one of the electric insect deterrents such as Vapa-Mat (both are widely available locally).

**Sea urchins** are common in rocky, coastal areas; if you are unfortunate enough to step on one, remove the spines with tweezers and douse the affected area with lemon juice, olive oil or ammonia (the most convenient source of which is urine). Ammonia is also an effective remedy for jellyfish stings.

British and other EU nationals can obtain free **medical care** under reciprocal EU arrangements, although

## GREEK ALPHABET

The Greek alphabet may look daunting at first, but it only takes an hour or so to memorize. A knowledge of the alphabet will enable you to read road and other signs, and the destinations of local buses. The chart below shows upper and lower case characters of the alphabet, together with a guide to the pronunciation of their Greek names.

| | | |
|---|---|---|
| Α | α | **ahl**fah |
| Β | β | **vee**tah |
| Γ | γ | **ghah**mah |
| Δ | δ | **dhehl**tah |
| Ε | ε | **eh**pseelonn |
| Ζ | ζ | **zee**tah |
| Η | η | **ee**tah |
| Θ | θ | **thee**tah |
| Ι | ι | **yeeo**tah |
| Κ | κ | **kah**pah |
| Λ | λ | **lahm**dhah |
| Μ | μ | mee |
| Ν | ν | nee |
| Ξ | ξ | ksee |
| Ο | ο | **o**meekron |
| Π | π | pee |
| Ρ | ρ | ro |
| Σ | σ | **seegh**mah |
| Τ | τ | tahf |
| Υ | υ | **eep**seelonn |
| Φ | φ | fee |
| Χ | χ | khee |
| Ψ | ψ | psee |
| Ω | ω | o**mehg**hah |

this covers only the basic standard of treatment. Emergencies will usually be treated free, but medical insurance against illness or accident is always a sensible precaution. Make sure that any policy you take out covers the cost of repatriation by air ambulance.

There are English-speaking doctors in most resorts and bigger towns (contact the Tourist Police if your hotel is unable to provide a contact number). For minor ailments you can try the pharmacy (*farmakio*, indicated by a sign with a green or red cross on a white background), which is able to dispense a wide range of medications. If you're on a regular prescription drug remember to bring enough supplies with you, plus a copy of the prescription itself in case of problems.

## Personal Safety

There are few problems with personal safety on Crete, although women may find themselves subjected to verbal harassment in resort areas where the myth of 'liberated' foreign women prevails. Cretan youths compete with each other over the summer months to see who can achieve the most success as a *kamaki* (literally, spearfisherman) and when they go home to their villages in the winter they add up their scores depending on the nationalities of their conquests. If this isn't what you had in mind, useful words include *stamáta* ('stop it'), *fiyete* ('go away'), and *afisteme* ('leave me alone').

## Emergencies

Dial 100, an all-purpose emergency number.

## Etiquette

Even in the big resorts, Cretans often remain genuinely sincere and friendly to foreigners. In the villages you may be offered hospitality which goes far beyond what might be expected.

In rural areas women should dress modestly, and bare shoulders and legs should be covered up whilst visiting monasteries. Topless bathing is now normal in resort areas, but away from these enclaves you should be discreet.

## Language

Most people in tourist areas and hotels speak English, but Cretans will be appreciative of your efforts to speak a few words of their language. A few basic words and phrases which are useful:

Yes *néh*
No *óhi*
Good morning *kaliméra*
Good evening *kalispéra*
Goodnight *kalinikta*
Please *parakaló*
Sorry/excuse me *signómi*
Thank you *efharistó*
How much? *póso káni?*
Where is? *pou ine?*
Today *símera*
Tomorrow *ávrio*
Yesterday *ekhtés*
My name is *meh léne*
1 *énos éna/mía*
2 *thio*
3 *tris/tria*
4 *tésseres/téssera*
5 *pénde*
6 *éksi*
7 *eftá*
8 *okhtó*
9 *enyá*
10 *dhéka*
20 *íkosi*
30 *triánda*
40 *saránda*
50 *peninda*
100 *ekató*
1000 *hilies/ia*
2000 *thio hiliádhes*

# INDEX

Note: Numbers in **bold** indicate photographs

Afráta 109
agriculture 22
Akrotíri Peninsula 101, 106–7
Almirós, Áyios Nikólaos 11
Almirós River 108
Amári Valley 88, 93, **94**
Ambélou, Pass of 71
Amoúdi Beach 97
Angathiá 77
animals 10
Anóyia 91, 93
Apodoúlou 93
Arabs 18, 19, 33, 76
Askífou Plateau 116, **117**
Ayía Ekateríni **40**, 41
Ayía Galíni 85, 88, 93, 95
Ayía Pelayía 45, **50**–51
Ayía Rouméli 101, 114–5
Ayía Triádha Monastery **100**
Ayía Triádha, Palace of 15, 39, 45, 55, 58
Áyii Dhéka 59
Áyios Giórgios 71
Áyios Ioánnis 109
Áyios Márkos, Iráklion 35
Áyios Nikólaos 11, 22, 63, 64–6, **65**
Áyios Nikólaos Archaeological Museum 65
Áyios Pávlos Beach 95
Áyios Títos, Iráklion **35**
Áyios Yióryios Beach 95
Azoyirés 113

Balí 90
Battle of Crete 21, 103
Battle of Crete and Resistance Museum 36
Bay of Pigs 97
birds 10, 11, 108, 114
Bronze Age 12
bull cult 14, 38, 57
Bull's Head Rhyton **14**
Byzantium 5, 18, 19

Cave of St John 107
charcoal-burning **90**
Christianity 18
climate 8
coffee 31
costume 26
Cretan Ibex see kri–kri

Cyrenaica 18, 59

Daedalos 17
Daliánnis, Hatzimichális 118
Damnóni Beach 97
dance 26, **27**, 104
deforestation 9
Dhamaskinós, Mihaílis 41
Dhaskaloyiánnis, Ioánnis 20
Dhía Island 40
Dhiktean Cave 16, 70–1, 92
Dhiktean Mountains 63, 67, 70
Dhrápano, Cape 108
Díktynna, Sanctuary of 109
Dorians 15, 18, 39, 59, 67
drinks 30–1

Easter 26–7
economy 22–3
Egyptians 21, 39
El Greco 41, 45, 51
Elafonísi 101, 111–2, **113**
Élos 111
Eloúndha 65, 68, 110
Énosis 20
Eteocretans 18
Europa 16
European Union 22
Evans, Sir Arthur 12, 15, 46–8, **47**

Falásarna 101, **110**
family life 24
festivals 25, 27
Firkas, Haniá 104
First Palace Period 13, 38
flowers 5, 8–10, 57, 93, 97, 114
Fódhele 45, 51
Fokás, Nikefóras 19
food 28–30
Fortezza, Réthimnon **86**, 87–8
Fourfourás 94
Frangokástello **118**–9
frescoes, Byzantine 63, 66, 72, 93, 94
frescoes, Minoan 14, **17**, **38**, **46**, 48, 58

Gaidouronísi 80
Gávdos Island 112, 119
Genoese 19, 102
geology 7
Georgioúpolis 11, 108, **108**
Górtyn 16, **18**, **19**, 35, 45, 55, 57, 59
Gourniá 15, 63, 72-3

government 22
Gramvoúsa 101
Greece 5, 21–2, 102
Greek Independence, War of 20, 118

Haniá 5, 15, 22, 86, 101–105, **103**, **104**, 114
Haniá Cretan Museum 105
Haniá Museum 109
Harvesters' Vase 39, **58**
Hersónissos 45, 52, **53**
hiking 113–**116**, 119
Hóra Sfakíon 114–119

Icarus 17
iconostasia **25**
Idean Cave 91–3
Ídha, Mount see Psilorítis
Ierápetra 7, 9, 63, 73, 80–**81**
Ímbros Ravine 7, 116
independence 41
Iráklion 5, 19, 20, 22–3, **30**, **32**, 33–43, 102
Iráklion Archaeological Museum 38–9, 43
Iráklion Historical Museum 40–1
Iron Age 18
Iron Gates see Sidherespórtes
Islam 20
Ístron Bay **73**
Ítanos 77

kafenía 30–1.
Kaló Chorió 72
Kalokairinós, Minos 46
Kamáres ware 38
Kastél Selínou 113
Kastélli, Haniá 104
Kastélli Kissámou 110, 111
Kástro Koúles **32**, 34, 40
Káto Zákros 75, **78**–79
Kazantzakis Museum 54
Kazantzakis, Nikos 37, 41, 54
Knossós 5, **12**, 13, 15, 17, 23, 38–9, **44**, 45–50, 56–7, 102, 113
Kókkinos Pírgos 95
Kolimbári 108–9
Kotsifoú Gorge 88
Kournás, Lake 6, 11, 108, **109**
Kourtaliótiko Gorge 88, 96
Kreipe, General 21, 91, 93
kri–kri 10, 40, 114

Kritsá **62**, 67
Kydonia 15, 102

labyrinth 17
Lasíthi Plateau **7**, 22, 45, 63, 69–71, **70**
Lató 67
Law Code of Górtyn 18, 59
leatherwork 64, 67, 86, 103
Lefká Óri (White Mountains) **6**, 7, 10, 26, 85, 101–2, 112
Linear A 13, 39, 75
Linear B 13, 15, 39
Loggia, Iráklion 35
Loutró 101, 114, 117
Lychnostatis Cretan Open-air Museum 52

Mália 13, 38, 45, 53
Mália, Palace of 53–**54**
Mátala 16, 45, **55**
Melidóni Cave 91
Méronas 94
Messará Plain 6, 45, 56–9
Minoans 5, 9, 12–14, 38–9, 45–51, 53, 57–8, 65, 73, 78–79
Minos, King 15–17, 47, 70
Minotaur 17, 48
Mirabéllo, Bay of 63–4, 71–2
Mirthios 97
Mírtia 54
Móhlos 72–4
Moní Arkádi 85, **89**
Moní Asomáton 94
Moní Ayía Triádha **106**–107
Moní Áyios Ioánnis Theológos 95
Moní Faneroméni 71–**72**
Moní Gonía 109
Moní Gouvernétou 106–**107**
Moní Hrysoskalítissa **111**
Moni Katholikó 107
Moní Préveli 85, 95–**96**, 97
Moní Tóplou 75
Morosini Fountain 35, 86
Mosque of the Janissaries **20**, 104
Museum of Cretan Ethnography 58–9
music 26, 104
Mycenaeans 15, 39, 102
mythology 16–17

Napoleon 81

# INDEX

NATO 21
Naval Museum, Haniá 104–5
New Palace Period 14, 39
Nídha Plateau 7, 93
nightlife 53, 64, 90

Oloús 68
Omalós Plateau 7, 114
Orthodox Church 19, 25

Palékastro 77–8
Paleóhora 111–14, 119
Palm Beach 85, 96–7
Panayiá Kerá 63, 66, **67**
Pánormos 90
peak sanctuaries 14, 38
Pérama 91
Phaistós 5, 13, 23, 45, 55–8, **57**
Phaistós Disk 38–9, **39**, 58
*pithoi* **5**, **48**, 51
Plakiás 85, 97
Plátanos 73, 110
Poseidon 17
Postpalatial Period 15
pottery 13, **16**, 38–9, 67
Prepalatial Period 12

Preveli Beach *see* Palm Beach
Psilorítis Range 6, 7, 45, 56, 85, **92**, 94–5
Psíra Island 73
Psychró 71

*rakí* 30, **31**
religion 25
Renieri Gate, Haniá 104
Réthimnon 5, 22, **84**, 85–8
Réthimnon Archaeological Museum 88
Rimondi Fountain 86
Rodhópou Peninsula 101, 108–9
Romans 5, 18, 33, 57, 59, 102

St John the Hermit 106
St Paul 18, 119
Samariá Gorge 5, 6, 7, 101, 112–116, **114**, **116**
Santorini 15, 65, 78
sarcophagi 14, 39, **75**, 104
Sarpedon 17
Schliemann, Heinrich 46
Sellia 97

Sfáka 73
Sfakiá 25
Sidherespórtes 115
Sitía 7, 63, **74-75**
snake goddesses 39
Sóudha Bay 106
Soúyia 114
Spinalónga Island 63, 68–**69**
Stavrós 107
Stone Age 12, 38

*távli* **29**
Theotokópoulos, Doménico *see* El Greco
Théra *see* Santorini
Thrónos 94
Tílissos 15, 45, 51
Titus 18, 35
tourism 23–4
Turks 5, 9, 20–21, 25, 33, 35, 40, '64, 69, 70, 75, 86, 89, 91, 96, 103
Tzermiádho 71

University of Crete 102

Vái 63, **76**-77, 85

Valley of the Dead 79
vendettas 25
Venetians 5, 9, 19, 26, 33, 35, 40, 68–70, 86, 102, 104
Venizélos, Eleftherios 20, 21, 107
Venizélos, Sophocles 107
Vizári 94
*vólta* 24
Vóri 58–9
Voulisméni, Lake 64–5

weavings 67, 86, 91, 103
weddings 24
windsurfing 112
wine 31
World War II 1, 25, 75, 91, 93, 96, 103

Yerakári 95
Yeropótamos, River 6
Yioúhtas, Mount **36**, 37

Zákros, Palace of 63, 78–9
Zeus 16, 37, 70–1, 92–3
*Zorba the Greek* 107